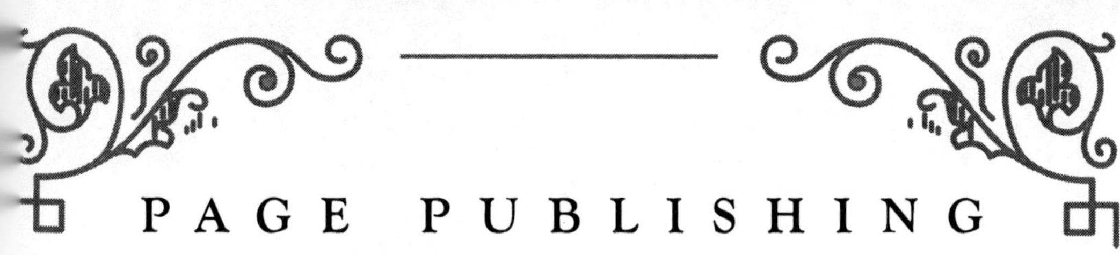

PAGE PUBLISHING

POETRY ANTHOLOGY

VOLUME 3

Edward J. Br

Brian W. Jerden Sr.

Michael Martinez

Nick Olsen

F.J. D'avino

Ray Springer

Sparkle Kenner

Messiah Brown

D.P. Parsons

Robert Watts Jr.

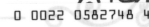

First Edition

PAGE PUBLISHING, INC.
New York, NY

First originally published by Page Publishing, Inc. 2018

ISBN 978-1-64298-368-5 (Paperback)
ISBN 978-1-64298-375-3 (Digital)

Printed in the United States of America

CONTENTS

Ancient! & Free!

Edward J. Bradley

To all U.S. Military Veterans and in commemoration of the annual American national holidays of Memorial Day (last Monday in May), Independence Day (July 4) and Veteran's (Armistice) Day (November 11).

https://www.booksie.com/posting/edwardjbradleysr/americathefree9096

America!, The Free!

Others may boast of their grand ancient cultures.
Their Books! Music! and Historical Ties!
Nations misled by tyrants and vultures.
Where liberty died! Due to treachery and lies.

America's environs wild! Where patriots always smile.
Blessed with abundance! Mean much more to me.
With sun, rain and cloud! Where fertile fields are plowed!
Home of the brave and proud! Land of the free!

*

Shining bright! From God's Holy Mountain!
Spirit of America! Fearless and Free!
Red, White and Blue! Waves o'er stream and fountain!
As strongly She stands! Watching over the seas!

Like Her frontier wild! She has serenely smiled!
When armies and empires! Against Her were hurled!
Hard! As Her Plymouth Rock! Absorbing ev'ry shock!
From Germany! Japan! and Terrorism's world!

*

All freedom has come from America's great courage!
Even for Her enemies! From prior war!
The rest of the world! Would still be in bondage!
With Hunger! Disease! Slavery! and More!

Brave patriotic tunes! Played over bloody tombs!
Red! White! and Blue! Still Her colors wave!
Salutes from rifles peal! For Her wills of steel!
Triumphant! On battlefield! America! The Free!

*

See how strongly! Her freedom's advancing!
Destroying all slavery! Found in its path!
Her sons and Her daughters! Like bright lights dancing!
Ignoring the stench of both ruin and death!

Brave patriotic tunes! Played over bloody tombs!
Red! White! and Blue! Still Her colors wave!
Salutes from rifles peal! For Her wills of steel!
Triumphant! On battlefield! America! The Free!

Triumphant! On battlefield! America! The Free!

https://www.booksie.com/posting/edwardjbradleysr/navygravy4099

Navy Gravy

Skin and Bone At Seventeen,
Left Home To Join The Navy.

All Muscled-Up At Nineteen,
Refused To Eat The Gravy.

Was Not Having That Much Fun,
With Hair Still Blond And Wavy

Went Back Home At Twenty-One,
Yelled: "Ahoy!" To The Navy.

https://www.booksie.com/posting/edwardjbradleysr/limerickforlife2916

Limerick for Life

Children StartOut In The Womb.
The Aging EndUp In The Tomb.

Destruction Of Either
Benefits Neither.

As Life For Both Ends Much Too Soon.

https://www.booksie.com/posting/edwardjbradleysr/thespirit3296

The Spirit

The Spirit's The Voice
Of Our Heavenly Father,
Hand Of Our Brother,
Jesus, The Christ.

The Spirit Watches
Our Struggles And Trials.
The Spirit's The One
Who Helps Us Do Right.

The Spirit's The Bearer
Of Good And Bad Tidings,
Vanquishes Darkness,
Brings On The Dawn.

The Spirit Gives Rain,
Then Creates A Rainbow.
The Spirit's The One
Who Inspired The First Poem.

The Spirit's The Builder
Of Cities And Highways,
Majestic Mountains
And Thundering Seas.

The Spirit's The Giver
And Taker Of Blessings.
The Spirit Attends Those,
Who Live Righteously.

Pray For The Spirit And
Blessings He Offers,
Follow The Prompter,
Whenever You're Called.

In Your Heart And Your Mind,
When The Spirit Dwells In You.
Bow Down Your Head And
Give Thanks To The Lord.

Children

https://www.booksie.com/posting/edwardjbradleysr/excitement
inspiredinhishertime7268

Excitement Inspired!

(In His/Her Time)
Let the Spirit that guides
Take you to where,

You'll be with others
For whom you care.

*

Hope all, whom you meet are
Not from a zoo

And all of them will
Care for you too.

*

Your College success!
Triumph! For you,

Hope it's not "Good-bye!"
Forever too!

*

Now! What will you do?
Where will you go?

Just once in a while,
Will you let us know?

*

When places afar can't
Make your soul burn.

Many! Right here!
'Wait your return.

*

Your future success.
Who can say "When?"?

"Long time, No see!".
"N'est tres bien!"

*

By Now, you must think:
"What a strange poem!"

From one far away.
But no longer know'm/r.

https://www.booksie.com/posting/edwardjbradleysr/poems1807

Poems

Poems Are Merely
Songs Without Music.

Songs Without Music
With Something To Say.

Poems Read To Your Children
Will Show Your Love For Them.

Bring Happiness To Them
And Brighten Their Day.

https://www.booksie.com/posting/edwardjbradleysr/apoem3847

A Poem

A Poem Is Merely
A Song Without Music.

A Song Without Music
With Something To Say.

A Poem Read To Your Children
Shows Your Love For Them.

Shows Your Love For Them
And Brightens Their Day.

https://www.booksie.com/posting/edwardjbradleysr/funnybunny5241

Funny Bunny

Funny Bunny
Was A Hare.

Funny Bunny
Always Scared.

Funny Bunny
Wasn't A

Very Funny
Bunny!
Honey!

https://www.booksie.com/posting/edwardjbradleysr/heretostay2395

Here to Stay

Edward J. Bradley and Mary Elizabeth Carroll

Mister/Miss **____________________**
Came To My/Our House One Day.
Not Just To Visit.
But Here To Stay.

Mister/Miss **____________________**
Sat And Ate Some Cake.
And Said, "What A Nice Home You Have,
But I Must Be Home Today."

Mister/Miss **____________________**
Finished Eating His/Her Cake.
And Said, "Thank You", Most Politely,
And Ran Home Right Away.

Mister/Miss **____________________**
Arrived Home Late That Day.
But Couldn't Eat His/Her Dinner.
Did Too Much Cake Get in The Way?

** - *Substitute The First and Last Name Of The Child To Whom You Are Reading.*

https://www.booksie.com/posting/edwardjbradleysr/youreawowforbabygirls4369

You're a Wow! (For Baby Girls)

Everybody Asks Of Me:
"Who's That Bundle Of Personality?"
We're So Proud Of You And How!
____________________!, You're A Wow.

Everybody Wants To Know:
"Where'd You Find That Lovely Cameo?"
We're So Proud Of You And How!
____________________!, You're A Wow.

Hear Them Whispering:
"Hasn't She Got Everything?"
You're A Stand-Out"
You'll Never Have To Ask A Hand-out!

We'll All Stand Up And Say:
"You're Our Presidential Candidate!"
We're So Proud Of You And How!
____________________!, You're A Wow.

** - *Use The First Name Of The Child To Whom You Are Reading.*

https://www.booksie.com/posting/edwardjbradleysr/youreawowforbabyboys4329

You're a Wow! (For Baby Boys)

Everybody Asks Of Me:
"Who's That Bundle Of Raw Vitality?"
We're So Proud Of You And How!
___________________!, You're A Wow.

Everybody Wants To Know:
"Where'd You Find That Handsome Romeo?"
We're So Proud Of You And How!
___________________!, You're A Wow.

Hear Them Whispering:
"Hasn't He Got Everything?"
You're A Stand-Out"
You'll Never Have To Ask A Hand-out!

We'll All Stand Up And Say:
"You're Our Presidential Candidate!"
We're So Proud Of You And How!
___________________!, You're A Wow.

** - *Use The First Name Of The Child To Whom You Are Reading.*

Humor

https://www.booksie.com/posting/edwardjbradleysr/changehaiku8518

"Change!" - haiku

"Change!" - Voters' pleading

Brings less that is good, while more

Taxes we're bleeding.

https://www.booksie.com/posting/edwardjbradleysr/longin
thetooth3084

Long in the Tooth

Rare
Are They,
Not Flattered
By Youth.

More
If Say,
When Long In
The Tooth.

https://www.booksie.com/posting/edwardjbradleysr/work8239

WorK!

"WorK!"
Just One More
Abysmal Day
Spent At WorK For
Little Pay!
*
"WorK!"
Tired And Sore
At End Of Day
"Shorter WorK-Weeks"
Some Might Pray!
*
"WorK!"
One More Way
To Kill A Day,
Feed Yourself With
Bills To Pay
*
"WorK!"
Just One More
Some Might Say,
An Exchange For
Dismal Pay!

*

"WorK!"
Just One More
4-Letter Word
Ending With The
Letter "K"!

*

https://www.booksie.com/posting/edwardjbradleysr/ourgrampaed5988

Our Grampa Ed

Rise and Shine ! With Grampa Ed.
Spends All Night & Day In Bed.
"Always Sleeping !" Someone Said.
Can't Awaken Grampa Ed.

No One Knows How He Gets Fed.
"Lives On Air !" Our Grampa Ed.
"He's So Lazy !" Someone Said.
"There's No Work ! From Grampa Ed."

Some Folks Say, "He Must Be Dead !".
They Don't Know Our Grampa Ed.
"Healthy Enough!" Doctor said.
"My Cash-Cow ! Your Grampa Ed."

Kept Us All Clothed, Housed & Fed.
"Who Knows How?" But Grampa Ed.
An Active Life ! Once ! He Led !
Now Too Tired ! Our Grampa Ed !

Once Awoke ! Found Himself Wed !
Back To Sleep ! Went Grampa Ed.
No One Tells How We Were Bred !
Neither Will Our Grampa Ed !

Most Romantic ! When Abed !

"They Find Me !" Claims Grampa Ed.
Had Five Wives ! They're Now All Dead !
Meant More Sleep For Grampa Ed.

Wars Were Fought ! Some Died and Bled !
Not The Case ! For Grampa Ed.
Much In Life ! Is Filled With Dread !
Noted Not By Grampa Ed.

"Current Events !" Must be said.
Inspire Not ! Our Grampa Ed.
Must Know Something ! Stays Unsaid !
"Make A Guess !" Says Grampa Ed.

No News Story Goes Unread.
Nothing Escapes Grampa Ed.
With Eyes In … Back Of His Head.
Hard To Trick ! Our Grampa Ed.

Sometimes gets hot. If instead,
We talk too much before bed.
"Knock-it-off ! Now ! Go to bed !"
Last words from Our Grampa Ed !

https://www.booksie.com/posting/edwardjbradleysr/selflove4465

Self Love

Loves Himself !
Thinks He's Grand !

At The Movies,
Holds His Own Hand !

Wraps His Arm,
'Round His Waist !

When He's Fresh,
Slaps His Face !

https://www.booksie.com/posting/edwardjbradleysr/saintpatrick
meetsclancy5489

St. Patrick Meets Clancy

St. Patrick Was A Saintly Man!
By All! Was Plainly Seen!

The Snakes All Drowned Themselves
With St. Patrick At The Scene.

He Never Looked For Serpents!
That's A Fact! We All Assume!

Nevertheless! When Serpents Would Press!
St. Patrick Lowered The Boom!

CHORUS:
Oh! St. Patrick!
Oh! St. Patrick!
Nevertheless! When Serpents Would Press!
St. Patrick Lowered The Boom!

https://www.booksie.com/posting/edwardjbradleysr/christmasditty
wethreekings4405

Christmas Ditty (We Three Kings)

We, Three Kings Of
Orient, Are
Puffing On A
Rubber Cigar.

It Was Loaded.
It Exploded……

We, Two Kings Of
Orient, Are
Puffing On A
Rubber Cigar.

It Was Loaded.
It Exploded……

I, One King Of
Orient, Can
See No Reason
To Smoke Again.

Merry Christmas!

https://www.booksie.com/posting/edwardjbradleysr/letwhatismeantbewhatissaid.odetowordsofonepulse5134

Ode to Words With "One Pulse"

If The Wrong Word Is Said,
In A World, Much Too Tight,
Then We Could All Be Dead,
With Folks Who Like To Fight.

Words We Use! Much Too Long!
As Few Know What They Mean.
All Can't Sing The Same Song,
With Words Not Known Or Seen.

Why Then? With Word And Pen.
Say Things Which When Are Sown,
Gives No Gain But Just Pain.
With Words Which Are Not Known.

If When Terse, With Our Verse,
And Brief With What Is Sent.
Our Good Will Does No Worse,
If What's Heard Is What's Meant.

Some Say, "To Speak This Way
Can Serve Us No Good Use."
But I Say, "Who Are They?
If At First, We Don't Muse?"

If Each Word, When It's Said
Means That Which Can't Be Known.
What's Said! When Heard Is Dead
And Sinks, Just Like A Stone.

In This Way, Hope To Say,
"One-Pulse" Words Make More Sense.
And "This World Will Be Great!"
When We Are All Less Tense.

You May Think, "All This Stinks!"
And Makes You To Feel Sick.
This Ode Ends In The Pink,
Mo-No-Syl-A-Boll-Lick.

Love

https://www.booksie.com/posting/edwardjbradleysr/friendsincloseharmony2167

Friends in Close Harmony

When We Make Music Together.
We're Made For Each Other.
We've Found We Can Be.
Friends In Close Harmony.

Now And Then, A Sour Note Is Sung.
Sour Notes! Soon Forgotten.
We Have Found, You See.
Friends Stay In Harmony.

Never Argue. Nor Do We Shout.
We Always Work It Out.
This Way, We Can Be.
Friends In Close Harmony.

Before The Sun Sets, Let Me Say.
"It Can't Be, 'nother Way."
Friends We'll Ever Be.
For We're In Harmony.

We Have Discovered We Can Be.
For We Have Found, You See.
Forever! We'll Be.
Friends In Close Harmony.

The Very Best Of Friends.
Friends In Close Harmony.

https://www.booksie.com/posting/edwardjbradleysr/katieanne3376

Katie Anne

Wonderful !
As Is She !
How Perfect Can
One Woman Be ?

Beautiful !
B'yond Belief !
Purloined His Heart!
Just Like A Thief!

Time Or Day,
Can't Be Told.
When Away !
His Heart She Stole.

Emotions Strong
Besiege His Soul,
Inspiring Poem
And Passion's Goal.

If His Kiss,
Would She Permit.
Could He Choose Where
First And Best
To Place It?

Nectar Sweet,
Would Taste Adore.
Awaits Him At
Her Ev'ry Pore.

Now Must Wait
Another Day,
To Know Her
Flavor And Bouquet.

Womanly !
Femin'Anne !
Most Divine !
Katie Anne !

https://www.booksie.com/posting/edwardjbradleysr/loveintended1235528

(In the style of a Shakespearean Sonnet (7 couplets of 14 lines of 10 syllables each))

Love Intended

For Whom! Among Them! Was I Intended?
Which Of The Women? Would Give Me Her Love?

If We Reached God's Ear! Could It Be Bended?
Would He Tell Us Dear?: "You Two! You're To Love!"

Had We Met Before? Or Cheated By Fate?
Were You Ever Mine? Tell Me! When and How?

School, Work, Church Or The Door? Now It's Too Late?
Is There Time Enough? For Each Other Now?

I'm Told, You've Been Near! My Lover And Wife!
Neither Did We See! Nor The Other's Scent!

Never Did She Appear! In My Lonely Life!
Hiding! Where Was She? Whom God Never Sent!

My Life's Been Ill Spent! Now Left All Alone.
If, To Me, You Appeared. You Were Not Known!

Epitaphs

https://www.booksie.com/posting/edwardjbradleysr/epitaph1inthissmalllife3236

Epitaph - 1 (In This Small Life)

In This Small Life,
Spent Much Alone.

Not Calm, But Strife.
To Most, Is Known.

Cannot Explain,
What Happened Here.

At Journey's End.
Can Peace Be Near?

Quite Often Heard,
When One Does 'st'itch.

And Fine'ly Now.
Has Found A Niche!

https://www.booksie.com/posting/edwardjbradleysr/epitaph2ifonlythey3268

Epitaph 2 (If Only They...)

Embraced His Death, With The Same
Great Passion And Enthusiasm

With Which He Sought Great Wealth, Fame,
Power and Beautiful Women.

If Only They
Had Come His Way.

https://www.booksie.com/posting/edwardjbradleysr/epitaph3somebones3986

Epitaph 8 (Malone's Bones)

Here Lie Some Bones!
Irene Malone's!
With Whom No Man Was Married.

Swindler! Whore!
Murderer! More!
Her Children Gladly Buried.

https://www.booksie.com/posting/edwardjbradleysr/epitaph4battyjones4085

Epitaph 4 (Baseball Batty.)

Here Lie The Bones.
Of Batty Jones'.
For Whom Life Held No Terrors.

Lived A Virgin!,
Died A Virgin!
No Hits, No Runs, No Errors.

https://www.booksie.com/posting/edwardjbradleysr/epitaph5wealth7710

Epitaph 5 (Wealth!)

When Young And Strong
His Legs Could Spring.
"Health!" To Thee He'd Sing.

When Old And Frail
He'd Ask - Not Sing
"Wealth! Where Was Thy Sting?"

Maranatha

Brian W. Jerden Sr.

I dedicate this book to Mrs. Roberta (Bobbie) Tipp, my college English Professor at Longview Community College. She kept alive my flame for writing. I told her, “writing was in my blood,” and she said, “writing is your blood”.

Everyone Cries

I know I haven't done much good,
Not doing good things I should,
So, I get on my knees and pray Lord please,
Forgive me so I can live free.

Everyone cries a few tears; some for love,
Some for joy, some for fear,
And the tears shed by me Lord,
Are from a sinner who's lost without thee.

In this wicked world where we live,
I remember your love so true,
Your promise of life for those who love you,
And death for those who don't.

Take Note

Monkey's chatter,
Cows moo,
Ducks quack,
Doves coo,
Pigs squeal,
Horses sound horrible,
But I can warble!

Flies hum,
Dogs growl,
Coyotes howl,
Frogs croak,
Bats screech,
Bees buzz tunes,
But I can croon!

Cats purr,
Lions roar,
Owls hoot,
Bears snore,
Sheep's baa,
Phones ring,
People say I can sing!

Journey

The world goes by in many ways,
To and fro, back and forth,
But do we stop to see?
Have we somewhere to go?

Trees sway lazily in spring breezes,
Birds dot here and there,
They too have places to go,
To us unknown.

A lady bug crawls along a window pane,
To rest its weary soul from strain,
Then suddenly takes flight,
Somewhere to go.

Clouds drift by in patterned splendor,
Drifting as the currents flow,
Never to last forever,
But now, somewhere to go.

Be thankful we can come and go,
Whenever we desire,
Be sure to carry peace and safety,
Through the morning and the night.

Peace Never Lasting

WARS!... Why?
Is it because we are barbaric? Since man existed, war has plagued our world. From the beginning of time, and even today. We have hot and cold conflicts that make no sense... or do they? God himself destroyed all but a few, by flooding the earth with water! Every war is our design, a result that's killed millions of people across the lands that He created. We are to blame for what we've done! Shame on us because peace on Earth will never happen until He comes again.

Renewed

As Jesus hung form the cross bleeding,
Our Lord looked far and wide,
As sinners watched him dying,
He prayed for everyone's soul.

God forsakes all the sinners,
His shed blood makes it so,
God knows all our weaknesses,
No matter how or where we go.

In pain He called out, "Forgive them,
They know not what they do."
He closed his eyes and breathes his last,
Suddenly our lives became renewed.

He's Coming Back

No man knows the day or hour,
When Christ the Lord will come in power,
But when He does, all heads will bow,
And knees will bend; that is His vow.

As promised with a trumpet blast,
Old Satan's power will end at last,
Jesus brings His kingdom here,
A new heaven and earth will then appear.

He's coming back, the Bible tells the story,
He's coming back in the twinkling of an eye,
He's coming back in power and in glory,
He's coming back with angels by His side.

United

With a world full of wars,
And patriots by the score,
Dying as they fight across the lands,
Let's find the peace we have not found,
Through the ages of recorded time.

We can save our lands or break them,
Nations can kill, mame, and end it,
It's up to each and every one,
Under God's golden sun,
to make freedom for the people of this land.

We must learn to live together,
As brothers and sisters,
Sharing and caring for each other,
Be a neighbor, be a friend,
And the fighting will surely end.

Ponder

Does anyone really know,
What life is really about?
The ends and outs, the highs and the lows,
We think we do but don't.

Where have we come from,
And where will we go?
From ape or God; for some,
Do we really know?

Is it truly that important?
To understand the reason?
Life exists and if we can't,
Accept the fact it does.

Be thankful for what you have,
And live life to its fullest,
For days will pass by quickly,
Til' Earth consumes our dust.

Happy go-lucky Guy

I don't need no worries,
Take away all my cares,
I feel as light as a feather,
Floating on air; I don't care.

Give me a little ol' tune to whistle,
Give me a song to sing,
I'm just a happy go-lucky,
Doing my thing.

I don't worry, I'm never in a hurry,
Let the whole world pass me by,
I'm just a happy,
happy go-lucky guy.

Power of Blessings

Once my life was filled with trouble,
Needing help and on the double,
I turned my heart to Christ the King,
Now I have a song to sing.

He gives me strength when I have none,
And does it with such compassion,
I'm no longer plagued with tears,
He has conquered all my fears.

God fills my heart with tender mercy,
And gives His blessings without ceasing,
When it seems I'm doomed to fall,
He quickly answers when I call.

Blessings bring joy and hope,
Filling you with power to cope,
Blessings are from high above,
They keep the blues on the run.

Almost Lost

Time has come for evil to dwell,
Throughout the world and universe,
The doors are opening to the gates of hell,
Spreading hate and greed, even worse.

You see it and smell it all around,
Taking with it; love, hate, and happiness,
I hear that distant trumpet sound,
Blasting forth a flume of darkness.

Grinding and gnashing of teeth you will hear,
In that hail of hot fire and brimstone,
Almost all are bound to fear,
But with God's love, we'll all be cleared.

Mourning Lisa

I remember her sweet touch and smile,
The way she looked into my eyes,
Now she's run away with my friend,
Her love is gone; all a lie.

Our love was deep walking hand in hand,
Little did I know the future to come,
I went crazy, couldn't understand
What went wrong; I felt so numb.

She was everything a man could ask for,
A pretty face, down to her lickable toes,
Her sexuality overflowed, making me sore,
But ended as the story shows.

My heart is broken, broken, broken,
Tears flood my swollen eyes,
Now I find my eyes wide open,
So I'll just say…Lisa…goodbye.

Understand

At first, we could not understand,
Strange feelings deep inside us,
In time, thoughts started to unravel,
We were different than most others.

As ages passed, our souls discovered,
It was a male he desired, and a female she wanted,
People said they were gay and not normal,
Why is it so labeled?

A man's heart knows how it feels,
As do women who find the rainbow,
All genders should live the life they're given,
In spite of those who can't understand.

Slow Down

Don't sweat the small things,
It brings only toil and fear.
That's not all it brings,
Sometimes anger, even tears.

Look for the small picture now,
What's so important it can't wait?
Hurrying makes you anxious,
Needing to be first out of the gate.

Slow down and ponder what,
Makes you sweat these things,
It's usually something trivial,
Heartache is all it brings.

It's time to look around,
Listen, learn, and slow down.
Then you'll realize just when,
It's time to enter the big race.

Pure Love

I can wait for the snow in the winter,
And the flowers that bloom in the Spring,
I can wait for the Summer and the colors of Fall,
But I can't wait for you.
'Cause my heart takes a beating just thinking of you.

They say we should love one another,
And my wish will always be this,
That you will be mine, til' the sun stops shining,
And the moon has no oceans to pull.

Love your partner with all your heart,
And your neighbors, as we do ourselves,
I hope you are mine, until the end of time,
Let love fill our hearts and minds.

Compassion

Once my life was filled with troubles,
Needing help and on the double,
I turned my heart to the Christ the King,
Now I have a song to sing.

He gives me strength when I have none,
And does it all with compassion,
I'm no longer plagued with tears,
He has conquered all my fears.

God fills my heart with tender mercy,
And gives His blessings without ceasing,
When it seems I'm doomed to fall,
He quickly answers when I call.

Spring View

Seagulls like snow covered mountains,
Dot the lake in early morning,
New foliaged trees strategically,
Line the distant shoreline.

Pulling nature forward,
Clouds of whispering smoke,
Grace the scenery above,
A perfect day for fishing.

Birds of a feather wing their way,
Pompously across the land,
Branches peek barren fingers,
Above the water's edge.

Big, green rocks of ages passed,
Lay beneath the liquid surface,
The fish aren't biting,
But spring is.

Neverland

We're starting over again,
New faces and places at hand,
A new house of wood, not sand,
In a beautiful, beautiful glorious land.

Surrounded with lakes and swimming ducks,
With tree's galore and sunsets adored,
Streets of gold showing our luck,
A place where no one gets bored.

A never, neverland one could say,
The new beginning in life we sought,
We thank God for this awesome day,
As we travel to the new home we bought.

Just Kidding

What's a poem without humor?
To make you smile and giggle,
To ease the stress and rumors,
And take away the wiggles.

There was a hungry lady,
Who took a ride on the subway,
Although she was shady,
She still didn't find a sandwich.

How about the pampered baby?
Who got everything she wanted,
Socks, shoes and toys galore.
Except she peed her pants; out of the diapers.

There was this man who sat up,
All night, wondering where the sun went,
He thought and thought
And finally, it dawned on him.

Expansion

What lies beyond our solar system?
Planets, moons, or aliens from other worlds,
Our universe holds many mysteries and surprises,
Don't think earth the only entity here.

Reports of alien abductions and experimentation,
Are heard around the world today,
Many have witnessed such phenomenon,
Makes you think it could be true.

Our government says it's fake news,
No proof of UFO's they say,
Because we've never uncovered a single craft,
That's why many doubt this topic.

Time has come to prove this mystery,
It shall be, but not by earthlings,
Instead, from aliens with a trumpet blast,
In the final days of Armageddon!!

2 a.m. Interlude Poetry and Epigrams

This is dedicated to anyone that is a victim of
love, broken promises and betrayal.
Take care.
Always,
Michael

MICHAEL MARTINEZ

She asked "do I ever cross your mind" I showed
my wrist and said "from time to time"

She doesn't do everything right, she has no spark,
she has no light, but she'll do for tonight

Lust and love like two sisters both so sweet, yet one's
so bitter for true love she'll never meet

Her goodnights felt more and more like goodbyes… or maybe good lies

I kiss your lips; I realize that it's over. Goddamn I wish I were sober

I'll never quite get it, I'll never understand, why
your words hurt more than your hands

How sad is it that we will never be… a modern day
Romero and Juliet but with more tragedy

My thoughts so deep I can feel my heart starting to drown

She was a social butterfly caught in his web of lies

Little did I know that she was already gone…
she was the queen and I just a pawn

You never looked more lonely… then around all your friends,
trying to figure out why all your love stories have a short end
She wanted distance and a new start; she was
my world but now we're planets apart

I wanna be on the same page but she started at
the end and I was somewhere in between

My days seem to drag, and my nights are so blurry
I think my friends are starting to worry

She could tell that I've been going through hell wondered when I'd come
back, she said, "Your heart so black from the affection you give back"

Lies lead to pills "I need to stop drinking" pills
lead to bed anything to stop thinking

Woke up to a text at 2:42, she wasn't you. But I guess she'll do

I'm a prisoner of my past, my future comes to visit,
offers a present but I never let it last

I guess that's just how it goes, scrolling through old pictures cause
you never know. Try to catch yourself when they let go.

She sat on my bed, hands covered in red, "a night with
the girls" is all that she said, tomorrow I'll just treat
her just like she was dead and leave her on read

These whiskey shots burn going down; the bartender
said, "I know it hurts when you're down, especially
when your phone doesn't make a sound"

So much for the magic, someone handed me a smoke,
for her final trick she asked for a mirror and coke

It shouldn't be this hard to love you, it shouldn't be this hard
to trust you, I shouldn't hate you every time I see your face,
but I do, you're the reason she left and everything has gone
wrong. This is why I hate staring in the mirror so long

I don't know what's harder to find, someone to trust or someone to love

I see the broken me in you, that's how I knew I found myself again

She's the player my hearts her game, I said, "I love
you" first. Her eyes said what a shame…

She tried to come back like a season 2 and
make things right, but she wasn't you

As I sit here so broken hearted, I wish I had ended it before it started

Pieces of my heart from the middle to the start and how it all fell apart

Put the blade to my wrist and let the blood flow, while I
have only a few moments to figure out why you let go

She threw dirt on her past, as she asked for
another double in a rocks glass

I wanna let go but I can't, this shot in my hand helps me understand why she left me for a better man

Bar full of flies hearts full of lies shots full of whiskey how many till she gets risky

She was my stars and I was her moon, we lit up the world, a love that almost ended too soon

It's crazy to think how those 3 words can change your life… I'm leaving you

Her kiss was a sin, I knew she'd be the end of me, she said lets just be friends and she became more of a frenemy

Odds against me stakes are high pop these pills and so am I

I always wanted to be something more but in her eyes I was such a bore

Lost and lonely I wish I was I sober, check my phone
one time… Can't believe that it's over

My anxiety my paint it won't go away, so I'll
lie to the world and say I'm okay

She might have loved me, but she loved her pictures
more as each "like" pushed her closer to the door

She told me "I still think about us, from time to time"
I think she was confused from line to line

Bad intentions get no sleep, he's a wolf dressed like
a sheep walking around with little Bo peep

The truth is you can't save me, I wanna drink you
away, it's your fault that my blue skies are gray

I'm trying to get better but this ten-dollar pill taste so
bittersweet and makes my knees feel weak, but I'll take
anything to forget you and forget those last few weeks

I'm so pathetic and it's easy to see not even something
as beautiful as death wants someone like me

Asked for your hand but all you gave me was your middle finger

My mom saw my tears her biggest fears came to light, she
knew darkness was coming prayed for me every night

You were my dream girl, my partner in crime but
you broke me apart as you snorted each line

Her heart on her sleeve, the devil on her shoulder she's
got pills in her bag, this night wasn't over

We crossed paths as our eyes locked mine said, "it's water
under the bridge that you burned down years ago"

This relationship got me feeling like were in a little boat
but with a heavy heart it's hard to stay a float

The smoke finally cleared not a sound was heard,
defeat was apparent, she was free as a bird

She was brighter than any neon lights, but
stayed high like strings on kites

If only we didn't have a past, then there wouldn't
be a reason for these doubles in the glass

I find myself jealous and I know it's insane, I don't know
what loves you more…my heart or my brain

Drinks get stronger cause you're sick of his lies, hold
those tears back, I can see in your eyes

You know that feeling right before they go, like the
longest goodbye but you're the last to know

I'm trying to find another you, but instead I found a new me,
with no sleep, drinking anything that's dirt cheap and every
night seems right, seems new, I guess drinking is a new you

I'm waking up in parking lots, with empty parking spots,
with this bottle of crown, my life is spiraling down

Her heart over the rocks, sweet like coke is how I'd describe her smile, her eyes told a story that was straight up no lie, but she felt empty like her glass, you could tell she wasn't the type of girl to drown her past

You said "I never meant for this to happen" but I guess that's how it goes, gave me back my heart but you had to take my soul

I need to go home, I need to stop drinking, woke up in a parking lot. Damn, what was I thinking

Drunk texting you late… cause I don't know how to let go.
My friends in the living room keep telling me lets go
Welcome to the after party

Summer almost over and so are we, I don't know what's colder these drinks or me

This old flame really left her mark, she set my world on fire… that smile had such a spark

She's taking shots almost every night, how can the man of her dreams leave her with sleepless nights

Seems like every love story was a shame but
the outcome, an oh to familiar pain

She's got butterflies in her stomach and whiskey on her lips

Look at the stars in her eyes I can see them falling for me

He was falling faster than shooting stars, but he kept
space between them, he had his heart stuck in bars

I used to let her walk all over me and for a
thousand miles I was in denial

An old flame left her with fire in her eyes… and
ashes where her heart used to be

I know your heart in the right place, but your
mind and eyes always seem to wander

I wanted to cut the tension with a knife, but I left it in
her back, now I'd do anything to get her back

———

Broke my heart to see you again, not because of
what you did but because of how you been

———

She's trying to be the one but caught up in all the fun, she wants to
be in love, she wants something more, oh shit! She forgot her keys
by the door; her friends are laughing, "hurry up you whore"
Don't let him compare you to pennies, nickels and even those dimes, he's
not making sense, you're a diamond, he lost, he doesn't want you to shine

———

He took that weight of her world; he put that weight
on you, all because he couldn't wait on you

———

Her cottonmouth kept her relationships toxic, but it was okay,
she has friends, she's in the zone, she kept them in the zone,
they weren't true friends, they just wanted her in bed alone

———

Seems like my mind wants to race my heart every night,
this marathon seems to drag from darkness to light

———

How did I let myself get to this point, you're at the edge of my bed,
devil in red, you...taste just like wine, I know you're not mine, but
you're just so damn fine, now he's trying to call you from his friend line

She painted the perfect picture with those
hands that always let me down

Your man always tripping and the bags under your eyes
said you were ready to go but the only thing running
was old episodes from your favorite TV shows

She was so driven, it's a shame... our relationship went one way,
looking back... was it me or she, that didn't want to stay

She wanted a kiss goodnight, but kissing made
it personal and it was nothing personal

Her words cut deeper than any knife ever could,
she left her mark like a blade does to wood

She's trying to find her better half, but those
empty wine bottles tell of a bitter past

She chased her dreams but could never catch a break and every
time she'd fall, it always felt like she jumped from a 10-story wall

You had high hopes, but he had his rope around your throat and
your friends saw you down, when you had your feet off the ground

You said you had a heart of gold, well I guess it's true…
now I know why fools like me fall for you

Now that we're alone… I've never felt so alone, while you're checking
your phone, I'm wondering "am I so boring, or am I really alone"

Our future was dim together; I guess that's
why we hung out under neon lights

I can't be the man I need to be with you in my life, I can't be
the man I need to be for her, for myself, for you… how can I be
done?? When I'm so undone, I'm hanging on by a thread, that's
connected to your heart… I'm watching it unravel as I fall apart

She made a wish on every falling star, not to fall again
and every birthday wish to forget his kiss

She wore all black, but I still see right through her, I wish
she would have wore all white but I wasn't Mr. Right

You robbed me blind… I didn't see you rob this golden heart
of mine, now I understand why people say, "love is blind"

I'll talk and write to you every night and day but
staying faithful… there is just no way

Her knight became a nightmare as he used
his sword to cut out her heart

I remember getting on one knee asking you to be mine forever…
but now I'm on both knees picking up pieces of my heart

The beautiful thing about a rose is how they show us that love
dies slowly and beautifully falls apart… and tragically you
can't save it either… no matter how much you want to

I found myself reading old love letters but lost
myself again when I put them away

I took a stroll down memory lane, reached a fork in the road and got lost in the pain, I tried to turn back but nothing was the same

Grabbed Alice by the hand, this wonderland was far from grand… I whispered in her ear, "we're all a little sad here"

She had a dream catcher above her bed, I guess she was trying to catch the man of her dreams and it wasn't me

I was the boy with the 2 a.m. eyes and he was the boy with the dreamy blue his roses were red and mine a shade blue kinda like me when I saw how happy he made you

She can't decide between Mr. Right and Mr. perfect because she's got bigger things to worry about… like what shoes to wear tonight for Mr. Wrong

Love is in the air and every time I see your face I find it harder to breathe… maybe I should stay away before you take my breath away

Inspiration from the Universe

I would like to express my gratitude and thanks to the Creator of the Universe, my family, closest friends for their continued support and encouragement.

I especially want to send a very special thanks and love to my daughter Kelsey the joy of my life and my future wife Heather.

NICK OLSEN

To Heather, you are the muse in my life.
The galaxy of love, **where I have searched**
so many places as a traveler of space and time to find my true love which I can truly call mine.
My search is complete, for I have found in you that one star in the heavens that I can claim as mine.
We map our course as we set sail through the Galaxy of Love, which has claimed so many hearts and ended so many dreams.
But in our Galaxy of Love, we shall nurture the place we call home as the Galaxy of Love ….
The Galaxy of Love that is nourished by the Milky Way.
Our galactic garden shall continue to grow with the fertile soil that allows our galaxy to grow among the many galaxies extended in the heavens.
The Galaxy of Love,
The Galaxy of Love,
The Galaxy of Love.

2012

2012 was the time of change. The mystery has been wrapped up in an enigma and the disappearance of thriving

Mayan civilizations to new beginnings a new calendar for the millennia. The self-doubt of our existence and fate of our continued lives.

Or is it merely the renaissance and birth for as we forge our existence, new discoveries, new nations, new galaxies new species. This is about the changes that occur as we are all inter connected.

Are you ready? Willing to experience the dynamic changes or will you join those who passed without a trace.

Rejoice in the renewal of the spirit of self and connection of our celestial souls in the universe

Inspiration

Inspiration, you came into my life from afar, like a lightning rod, another plane of existence.

Inspiration, you've blessed me with these words, infused and interconnected in my mind like a superhighway to the galaxies, where encouragement and love prosper.

Inspiration, your words and feelings; created by the Universe and existed since the beginning of time, provide meaning and a frame of reference for us all.

Inspiration, I graciously accept the responsibility of delivering your messages and to share the happiness which grows deep in our hearts, our minds, and our souls.

Inspiration, you truly have inspired me to share your words of wisdom, to invoke change, share happiness, and promote love.

Inspiration, I am your Samurai, serving the community of Spirit!

Nirvana

Nirvana. Purgatory. Heaven. Hell.
Is all we see reality or personal choice?
Our free will allows us to choose our path.
Which will you take?

Lifted

If what we say can lift others to new heights,
Reciprocity creates the bond of togetherness,
And, we become the recipient of many blessings from above.

Eternity

We search, we seek, and we find the one we love.
The Almighty has predetermined this.

No matter what paths taken, our lives will intersect,
In the continuum where we discover our love.

As the cosmic forces directly intervene,
Our blessed union will become one spirit for eternity.

Roll Call

Just showing up doesn't necessarily mean,
You've met all goals and objectives.

Showing up actually means "showing up."
Showing up is the embodiment of the trinity of mind, body, and spirit.

Showing up for the sake of showing up is certainly NOT what our creator did when he SHOWED UP.

Stand up, put your shoulders back, and show up!
We all will benefit.

The Unbreakable

We may feel broken, like a glass fallen from the cupboard.
We are the unbreakable created by the Almighty,
Forged by his love and stamped as blessed.
With an endorsement like that,
You can never break!

Seasons

The Fall in your Life can be the longest Winter
or the Spring in your step that leads to the Brightest days of Summer!

Reframed

A reframed life is not one of distorted dreams painted in abstract.
It can be a picture of the blessed things to come.
When you look upon your own life, HOW do you frame your reality?

If

What if we dared to evolve from our fathers before us?
What if we dared to developed abstract thought and word?
What if we dared to take a chance on life and love?
What if as you ponder and answer your WHAT IFS, they become turning points in your life?
Open your heart to receive the answer to WHAT IF.

No?

If the NO in our life was definitive and absolute,
Then how could we have evolved thus far, even though our creator blessed us with free will?
To the Creator of the Universe, NO means I will NOT quit.
How will you respond to the NO in your life?

The Compass

If your compass draws you closer to what attracts you most, like positive ions,
Staying the course will never misguide you.

Allow the ionic forces to guide your compass true north!

DNA of Spirit

If strands of DNA determine our genetics,

The DNA of Spirit allows each of us to contribute our unique attributes of DNA to the fabric of the universal community.

What gifts will your DNA bring to our Community of Spirit?

Come together. Complete the strand.

The Outcome

Has our outcome been determined by what others think, or have you determined your outcome in life?

Do not let the thoughts of others sway what you think inside.

The outcome, in its pristine state, is determined by the change in yourself.

Own the outcome and be determined until you make it yours.

Sunrise to Sunset

Sunrise signifies a new day, fresh starts, do-overs, and retries.

Our sunsets rejuvenate, reinvigorate, refresh, and renew.

To some, it's simply repetition, like a stationary bike, to others, hope and new beginnings.

From sunrise to sunset you can either think or take action.

What are you waiting for?

Carpe diem.

The Invisible

Are we really invisible or did our community create it for the ME?

As a society, are we willing to shun our brothers and sisters as invisible for the sake of ME?

If we continue, we all appear invisible to the naked eye.

Recognizing others with mercy and compassion will lead us to brighter days.

The Book

If your life were a book, would it be a tragedy, a comedy or an inspiration?

Tragedy may seek pity from the observer and comedy will make us laugh,

But inspiration motivates generations to aspire to greatness.

Greatness

We are not put on this earth to settle for mediocrity.

Find your passion, get inspired,

And fulfill your aspirations of greatness

The Healing

Healing is the transactional agreement between mind, body, and soul.
Making the conscious decision to heal begins the process.

To forgive.
To live.
To love.

When

When is *when*? It's more than an open-ended question.

It could be a passing thought, or a turning point in our lives.

It could be a reaction, a call to action, or the one thing that propels us forward.

"When is when," could take a lifetime to discover, or it could happen this instant.

The choice is YOURS.

Attention

Attention is one thing. Creating tension is another.
Is a smile on your face worth the grimace on others?
Is that attention worth the tension?

Vindication

Vindication is the transparency of self without conjecture or promotion.

It allows others to speak for you when truth is sought about the purity of your heart.

The sweet sound of silence is golden, isn't it?

The Power of One

The Power of One is the spiritual alignment between your mind, body, and soul.

As we align these elements, we become the benefactors of this unification with the Universe and its blessings.

Potential

Potential is the untapped ability of self, which has been gifted to us from above.

With that gift, how can we miss fulfilling our destiny?

Potential is a promised gift waiting to be unwrapped.

Forgiveness

Only when you find forgiveness are the missing pieces of your heart filled.

And you start anew, your life complete.

Rebirth

As we embark upon our life path we all face trials and tribulations.

We either wither under the strain or conquer our fears.

As we cleanse our past, our soul will lead us into our promised land.

The Constitution

The newness of your surroundings does not constitute a fresh start.

When you surrender yourself to the Universe,

You allow for a fresh heart.

Innocence

We are born in purity and innocence. But are raised by a hypocritical society.

We are given free will by the Universe to choose our path.

Find innocence and purity to enrich your life.

Bright Lights

Don't let the smoke and mirrors of an event cloud your ability to make a decision that's right for you.

Let the clarity of perspective guide you through.

Crossroads

Jumping-off points, detours, and crossroads.

Jumping-off points lead to new directions in one's life,

Detours are distractions we take to lose our self.

Being at a crossroads is an opportunity to make a conscious decision to accept responsibility for our own actions.

Voice

When we find our voice, we allow our self to grow, to stand up and succeed, to ask for what's needed in the fulfillment of one's true self.

Direct, inspire, teach one another to find their Voice, and you'll find the Voice within you.

Shine

When you act the part, your ego talks,

When you are the part, your true self shines!

Reflection

When we reflect on our self what is it we see?
Do we see a friend or foe?
A foe's reflection is fear, anger, and self-doubt.
A friend's reflection is the true depiction of our inner beauty and loving self.

Bloom

We experience many seasons in our life. Seasons of growth, stagnation, anger, happiness, and love.

It is in a season of happiness and love we realize our greatest growth and bloom into the blessed being that the Almighty created in us.

Make this your season to grow and bloom.

Faith

Faith and hope are sparks that become the catalyst for our life that we dream and wish for.

But belief in our mind, belief in our heart, belief in our soul are the eternal flames which affirm our destiny.

Run

If we run from troubles and tribulations, does that mean our soul carries the burden?

It is the soul that stands tall and becomes the beacon of our success.

What illuminates from your soul, will radiate within and shine upon our lives.

Aperture

In seeking clarity of the mind, body, and soul,

The sharply defined supports our desired view of life.

The undefined leads us to see only what's in the foreground and not what's in the distance.

How will you set your aperture to achieve clarity?

Ready, aim, click.

Reality

We all share reality, only our viewpoints differ.
Some may call your view insanity.
Others may call it indifference.
Does standing in the middle make you normal?
Or just undecided?
Where do you stand?

Success

Success is the conceptualization of one's dreams,
The dreams that have become reality.
Will you dare to dream?

The Crossroads

The crossroads of life are upon us.
Our fate in life is determined by the direction we take.
At the crossroads, our journey can be through nirvana or hell.
Via con Dios!

Bravery or Principal

If bravery is the reaction to circumstance,

Then principle is the conscious decision to do what's right,

When you have time to think from the heart.

Love and Forgiveness

Love and forgiveness are the keys to restoring a healthy soul and loving heart.
The next move is yours.

Open the door to new beginnings.

Simplicity

Don't let the complexity of today's life,
Dismiss the simplicity of one's love for life.

The Muse

The Muse is a magical force, the divine, and integrated into the universe for us all.
The Muse is here to help us create, to express, to share, to love, and to be inspired.

The Muse in its abstract is the inspiration that ignites the creativity in our souls.

The Muse is a part of us all; it breathes life from the ethereal plain of the universe.
Are you ready to create and listen?

The Muse in your life may be calling.
Are you listening?

Yesterdays and Tomorrows

If yesterday held us back,
Our today bring us new life,
And a better tomorrow.

Burdens

Guilt and burdens are the shackles that weigh down the heart, mind, and soul.

Forgiveness is the key that alleviates and allows the spirit to soar free and rise above.

Barriers

It takes a lot of love and understanding to change the minds of some.

Patience is the best weapon to break down barriers in front of us.

The Navigator

As the navigator in your life, you guide and anticipate the safest direction.
Captain and guide your journey in life to safe harbor.

Friendships

Friendships have no expiration date,
Unless you have soured inside.
Stay fresh with the right nutrient,
Love!

Life

Our life does not end when we perish.

Our life lives on as friends and family continue to love us.

Honor, cherish, and love each other.

That is Eternity.

The Eternal Warrior

The Eternal Warrior has lived many lifetimes.

It has been born and reincarnated throughout the continuum and evolution of the warrior spirit.

The warrior spirit that breathes life to sustain the everlasting movement of peace through war.

The warrior spirit and its adornment, by its mere brute force, for those who cannot as the savior of civilization and yet feared in its own dichotomy.

We've honored and loathed the warriors for their deeds, but love the outcome for its glorious liberation

We honor you, Eternal Warrior.

We honor your feats, Eternal Warrior.

We honor your sacrifice, Eternal Warrior.
We honor you, Eternal Warrior.

Locked up

The thoughts that crowd my mind have been locked up for so long

Thoughts entrapped deep traveling throughout each synapse inside me

Locked up like an enigma clouding my judgement in my daily life

Locked up but looking for that key for my salvation

Locked up but with mercy and forgiveness I shall release me

Dividends

If the list you keep of did-me-wrongs and why me's

Your list will never end, and time spent operating in a deficit will bring a positive balance

Spend your time in earnest reflection that pays your way to a grand future

The Island

The island in confinement where the photosynthesis and nutrients revolve

The Island in confinement can draw only the nutrients in its ecosystem

The island that benefits from winds of prosperity is dependent upon the direction of the wind

But the islands in the stream together can garner life from sustenance of everlasting life

Your island but where the winds take you

Revolving Door

The rhythm of a revolving door resonates as it spins round keeping you in entrapped in your surroundings
That sense of ease walking thru a revolving door and its lure returning back where you started
We, at times, feel our life as the revolving door returning to back in comfort
If by chance, we step out of the revolving nature of habit and seek what brings light to your new world
And bring resolve to what we no longer want to revolve around us

This Time

If we continue to dwell on our results of " last time?
We leave "no" room and allowance for " this time"
Our "last time" is what we learn from
Our "this time" is the gift to embrace as a new beginning
Now, this time is your time to shine

One Day

One day, I will
For that one day is now
When will your "one day" arrive?
You'll be glad you did that on that "one day

Until We Meet (Again)

Good night sweet Angel until we meet again.
For we have met many times in many different lives
Our first meeting as two celestial souls searching for our nirvana.
We traveled different paths, but we find each other in the ether
While never saying goodbye to one another…
We simply say " until we meet again"
Our love for each other never fades but rekindles the moment we meet again
As our time together continues throughout the Universe,
we must not forget the precious time we've shared together
At times we come upon the winter years of our lives,
we merely say " until we meet again"
It is this journey my sweet angel that I remind myself that this is " not" goodbye
But, a very short slumber my sweet Angel
Until we meet again

Deception

Deception is the deed of the weak who lean on the backs of surrogates to acquire knowledge they lack

Deception is the hustler skilled in "three card monte" lacking the integrity of an honest days work

Don't be fooled by the slight of hand or swag of tongue for it is you that has been played by those who call you friend

Pilgrimage

For I have traveled along the trails of loneliness and despair yearning for reprieve and sanctity

What I have found in my quest the answers I seek resides in your heart

For it is the freedom, Love in our hearts where the spirit soars to your pilgrimage

Represent

Present what you represent for it's that shade you cast upon what shines bright

Don't confuse the tarnish upon my wares as patina to increase its value for your eyes purview

It may be the shade which the righteous man may see only to discover what a little varnish may improve

Shining bright day in day out with transparency for what the truth in your heart can see

They will know you present what you represent

Stars

The orbit in its existence consist of many stars and elements abound to sustain my surroundings

The nutrients in my orbit that replenishes life each day are the stars that shine bright in my eyes, my heart and my soul

For these stars are my guiding light and remind me of how bright the future will be

Shine on

Hanging around

Hanging around for my train to arrive

Hanging around for that train with thoughts swirling around to what lies ahead

Hanging around for that train to arrive to fulfill my accomplishments and destiny

Hanging around, just, hanging around for my adventure is about to begin

Seize the day or hanging around

The Burning Bush

For mine eyes have seen the destruction of the soul

For mine eyes closed have seen pain and hopelessness
in my soul

for mine eyes, I am blinded by own actions for sake of my flesh

for mine eyes, mine eyes, mine eyes for they blurred by haze that clouds self and direction

for the light from the burning bush will be my awakening to a future with mine

eyes wide open deep into my soul where the healing power of our creator

May the "burning bush" deliver you to salvation a life Anew

Remember

Remember those cherished days without a care in the world

Remember the innocence of childhood drinking from the hose

Remember the smell of fresh cut grass

Remember coming home when the lights come on

Remember?

Humble Pie

The desire and hunger for revenge will leave you wanting more

When you've expensed your own capital to feast

Only to afford a slice of humble pie

Homeless

Homeless is the empty heart that yearns to be filled with the love lost

Homeless is the heart sees no sustenance to feed the soul

Homeless is the heart knows no warmth from a simple embrace

Homeless is the heart that thirst for a refreshing conversation

I am homeless in mind, body and spirit

I pray I see the cornucopia of my thanksgiving and rejoice the sanctity of life

Whispers

Will the whispers of untruths drive the uncertainty and fear in your heart

Or the truth in your heart speak louder than faint whispers of pettiness

Your strength and resilience in your heart will overcome the lessor

Or the truth in your heart speak louder than faint whispers of pettiness

Pieces

Pieces of me, pieces of you separated by one that fits into the backdrop of life

Pieces of you and pieces of me a culmination of different shapes, sizes and vibrant colors

Pieces of me and pieces of you in its entirety completes this masterpiece for all to share

Come Home

Come home, come home where your heart lives where love dwells

Come home, come home thou you have journeyed on many paths only to yearn where you belong

Come home, come home for are never too far to feel the comfort and joy

Come home, come home for I will receive you with love in my heart and open arms

Come home, come home

Fact

Fact you, no fact you, no more are the facts the facts for the facts are swayed to make you believe their facts

But in essence, it's an agenda that fills these facts believed to be truths for an unthinkable mind satisfied to hear someone's truth than to seek your own

What say you… will you be brave and seek your own facts for "your" truth

As a matter of Fact

See of Red

See of red, sea of red I see red before my eyes the color red

On the endless beaches covered in red I see the sea of red for its deep color red in that see of red

I see the sea of red as it reminds me of how we fought centuries in that sea of red

What say you in that see of red for that sea of red is our freedom and thank those we lost in that sea of red

I hope you see the red reminding you the sea of red was paid with body and blood

God Bless those we will see in our hearts in that sea of red

Spin

Spin is how you apply to your own narrative or for "your" clarity

But if your spin is only to satisfy your ego to cleanse what dirt you desire to cover

Then "that" spin is merely cosmetic for the blemish on your ego

The only spin we so desire is the clarity from the heart

Truth!

Fear Uncertainty Doubt

Fear-Uncertainty-Doubt. The nomenclature that shutters the faint of heart
who navigate their daily lives seeking safe harbor

Fear stifles us

Uncertainty deters us

Doubt prevents us

To aspire to your greatest glory

Be **Fearless** in your decision

With **Uncharacteristic confidence**

And be **Determined with** courage to do what's right in your heart

Break that glass ceiling for you know no bounds

Alive

I feel alive as the sun shines bright on my face
I feel alive as the clouds provide the shade that keeps me cool
I feel alive as the rain washes my tears away on one of those days
I feel most alive when look into your eyes
Your eyes are the key that opens my heart and brings happiness to my soul
That's when I feel alive

Son

You came from the heavens in such delight
Your spirit shines as you travel through the Universe at the speed of light
Your seed was planted in the fertile garden to bloom and grow with all your might
For one night born unto your cornucopia of unconditional love and understanding
You will reap the rewards of this harvest o plenty
For you are the son that brightens the world

The Lonely Lamb

The suffering and sacrifice by ONE is enough to know how special we are

Share the joy to that lonely lamb who needs the comfort of its heard…Your gentle words

The Fisherman

Your greatest glory may not be the largest catch

But a blessed moment we share with our brothers and sisters

Everlasting life

Heather

She is God's creation, hair like freshly spun silk, skin soft as satin and body molded to perfection.

Her smile is warm and inviting to the strangers eye, makes those feel like they've arrived home a journey so long.

But with her smile… it brings back the remembrance of great times we had.

She is kind, loving and understanding like the forgiving mother who cares for her brood.

She is the woman that fills your heart with the warmth and loving spirit

She is God's blessing to us all

Amphibious

You may feel like the fish out of water like many before

It never stopped the amphibians to grow their legs and explore a new world

Step by step they evolved and conquered

We can too

Genuine

The genuine nature of one's heart is a true depiction of a generous soul
filled with acceptance and unconditional love

Instrument

The instruments used in battle to keep the rhythm in battle

Sound your horn, bang your drum, for it's your life and the way you prepare to succeed

Your beat, at your pace, forward march for your victory is upon you

This is me as I am

This is me brought into this world eyes wide open

This is me daughter, sister and friend

This is me in transition from adolescence to adulthood

This is me finding independence in my own thought

This is me whom I know inside but seen different

This is me asking to be accepted not judge nor compared

This is me learning from society and its complexities

This is me wanting to be the me I've wanted to be

This is me who wants to be accepted as me without judgement

This is me who wants to be appreciated for the person I am

This is me who wants to be loved unconditionally

This is me as I am

When our eyes met

I came into this world only to see this beautiful woman down upon me

Our eyes met starring into each other's eyes in adornment

This kind and nurturing woman holds me gently caressing my face

I wonder who this person is
She tells me that she will always be there for me

She tells me "I am your Mother and forever your friend"

Represent

Present what you represent for it's that shade you cast upon what shines bright

Don't confuse the tarnish upon my wares as patina to increase its value for your eyes purview

It may be the shade which the righteous man may see only to discover what a little varnish may improve

Shining bright day in day out with transparency for what the truth in your heart can see

They will know you present what you represent

When I look into your eyes

When I look into your eyes, I see the innocence and purity

When I look into your eyes, I see a boy looking at the world with amazement and curiosity

When I look into your eyes,
I see the blessed gifts by the almighty

When I look into your eyes, I see your opportunity and favor

When I look into your eyes, I see your accomplishments and victories

When I look into your eyes

The City Migrant

The city migrant never leave for it is truly the city that never sleeps.

We are up with both the eagle and the owl some just never sleep

The migratory pattern is never the same. We train, subway taxi and uber, walk run and rent a bike.

We lead our own flock we nest for the day, we flee at a moment's notice and fly like bats at sundown and find our way

We rely on ourselves for it is our "own" pack to care about for our salvation and peace of mind

The city migrant flies to its own destiny and never sleeps

Music

If music is the on ramp to another plane of existence and the stairway to heaven…

Then, a choir of Angels is the key that opens the gate to "usher " you into your glory

Brother

You were my first friend
You were my first adversary You were my first mentor
You were my trailblazer in this journey called life
Thou, our journey had taken separate paths but we found our way
One thing for sure, I am blessed to have a brother like you

Communique to Dad

Even thou the years have passed, and your life's journey ended on earth

I realize that it's only the beginning of your spiritual development.

Learn your lessons well for your work has just started in heaven as an angel

I, for one, learned from you that nothing is given to you. Hard work prevails and it's OK to celebrate tears of joy

I am writing this communique sent upon the wings of angels delivered to St Peter

Dad, I thank you for all those life's lessons you taught me

It has made me the person I aspire to be

Your Son

The Paradigm

I can't, I won't, I'll try

I will, I did, I conquered

Amazing how words we choose determine the outcome

Outcomes are determined by the paths we take

It's your path but which road will you travel?

Life of a Passerby

F.J. D'avino

Angels Don't Sleep

Night swept the day away
Sleep I needed badly
No rest in sight
As I stumbled through
The night
I prayed
A restful place
For my body to lay
And heal the wounds
Inflicted this day
Angels appeared, held
My hand,
Lifted me gently, and laid me
Down
Deep sleep overcame me
And
When I woke rested and peaceful,
No angels were in sight
I pushed away my
Fright
And cried out with much
Delight
Thank you winged friends
You have saved
This one's
Life

Blue Lady

Little one so blue, you
Ask, "where are
You"
Heartache and pain accompany
Thy name
But
Your love once given is
Boundless without
Shame
Many will exclaim, "I
Am here"
Open your heart, look
Deep inside, and you
Will see, they
Disappear
Meaningless journeys to
Find someone wasted time,
For
No true one will appear
You yourself are the
One you seek
Body to body is not
Love but a
Compromise
Love is the soul and
Spirit of your
Heart
Embrace this, and
True love will evade you not

Devils Are Real

All devils do not only exist
In darkness
Yeah
They live and bask in the sunlight
They do
Reaping the very soul of the innocent
From those who trust
Heed not their words for they lie
Slithering they are serpents
Poised to consume
And possess your soul
Denying
Your entry to heaven
Unless you pay
Their toll, if
Not,
To hell you go
With the loss of
Your soul

Family

Born of blood, rich in
Courage and goodness
Tasting life from past
Generations
Birthdays, holidays,
Every day
We were loved and
Protected by mother and
Father
Embraced by grandmother and
Grandfather
Time has taken them
It now belongs to
Us
To pass on the value of life as we
Have been taught
Take this time, embrace
The ones you love, and
Share with them as always
The greatest gift
Ever given mankind . . .
"Family"

Final Embrace

Violet shadows engulf
And capture the
Night
Eclipsing the light as
It fights to protect
Its right to be
Bright
Light disappears, I have
No sight
For
The spirits have surely
Risen this night
Searching and wondering,
Accompanied by
Fright
Consume my soul, if you must,
Oh shadow spirit
For I say to thee
In the end
We will embrace
Each other as
Dust

First Time

She moves toward me
As if on a cloud
Every movement of her body
Seduces me deeper into
Submission
My eyes riveted to her
Nakedness
Sinfully overwhelmed by her
Beauty
Speechless, word evade me
As
Her hands explore my body
Unparalleled ecstasy consumes
Me
We surrender to each other in
This moment of time
My virginity accepted, she
Whispers words of love
And assurance
While engaging me where
Only I have been
Lost in her world, my
Youthful innocence
Erupts
Soft lips meet into mine
Can't think, breath quickens,
Breast to chest, I loose
Myself again
She guides me, I taste
Her being
Silence is broken with
Moans of pure passion
Uncontrolled movements fire

Hot feelings, unlimited ecstasy
Now prevail
Cast your spell on it
This is my first, and pray God not
My last
I have passed
Love's test with great
Response
I will hold
This beautiful day deep in my heart
Forever
I have experienced
Love
And
Become a man

Fool's Work

Power, Money, Position
We all strive
Born with that embedded
And stamped in
Our mind
When all is done and
Your cup does runneth
Over
Say what is next
To digest
More of the same
Which
Will cast a bigger shadow
Of shame
Upon your name
A great man once said,
The pursuit of worldly goods is
Fool's work, which is never done
Nothing, nothing means anything
Except this result
I say again
God, health, and family
For all else is
A video game

Gifted Women

Willow tall, statue
Of unparalleled
Beauty
Your skin of velvet
Flawless and soft to the touch
Strength of character, loyalty
Bound by friendship
Boundless universal energy
Yet calm
Gifted fragrance exudes
An intoxicating scent
Possessing unparalleled passion beyond
One's limit
Giving all of self,
Defending friendship and love,
Sacrificing feelings of one's
Own heart
To secure the final
Embrace
And beyond time
Forever

God Bless America

Will any one called to duty
By his country
Be ever forgiven by man
Or God
For taken lives in the
Name of honor
And peace
Innocent and unknown to
Each other both feel
The same guilt
Man against man both
Love their God, families,
And the country they
Come from
Fight for your country
They say, "A hero you
May be"
Kill this man, he is
Your enemy
For honor and peace,
God will forgive
You
"Thou shalt not kill" in
The book it is
Written
How then can the Lord
Ignore His words that
He has scribed,
And
Forgive us for taking
Other's lives
Learn to forgive yourself,
So you can live

Day by day
See the faces of those
You have taken away
Love your country,
Obey God, do your
Duty, be a boy scout,
Altar boy, child of
Christianity, live by the
Law of God,
And
A shiny new metal
Will be bestowed on you
When you kill for the
Red, white, and blue

Hidden Love

Love if hidden is not
Real
But a plaything of
Truth to steal
Only once in a lifetime
Does love occur
Real and sacred a
Gift for ever more
Love makes one never
Forget
Moments of pleasure as
Well as regret
One's heart has only
Room for what love
Gives for being true
Be true to thine heart
The chamber of which
Holds love
For
Love if true is a
Gift from above
When alone and your love
Has left
That pain you feel is
Your heart breaking

Inner Space

There exists a peaceful place
Time it takes to find prepare
The journey
Do not make haste
Slowly transform your mind toward
The light
So no one can trace your sacred path
To your entrance of precious
Moments and thoughts in
Your special place
If you choose to take one along,
Make certain they share the same
Dream as you and no one else
Alas
For only then you will find
Love in your inner
Space

Love's Forgiveness

Speak to me not
Words that cut
Like the sharpest
Blade
But true and honest
As day to night
Leave me you say
For another
Pray the reason why
For
My life I have
Pleaded to you until
No light I can
See and air no
Longer I
Breath
No answer can you give
To satisfy my soul
For
With love comes
Forgiveness
Punish me for harm I
Have done
Not
For what I have
Not
Give my life back
To me

As you give yours
To another which once
Was mine alone
Depart if you must
Take my heart and
Love with thee
For no more will
I need
My pledge and vow to
You I have
Kept
Hear my last words
Painful my heart
As it may be
While you leave and
Give your love to
Another
To you my only
Love
I say
"I forgive thee"

Man to Man

Listen all you so-called
Men
Bet you a million to
One,
Neither you or I can do
Or endure
What women go through
We label them princesses
And then queens
They wink and slink, get
Married in a blink
God chose them to bear
Our children
Knowing with men, there
Would be none
Every month for most of their
Lives,
At work or play, part of
Them flows away
Enough pain and some so bad
That any man would
Wave the surrender
Flag
Remember, men,
They are your mothers, wives,
Sisters, lovers, caregivers,
And other
For this and so much more,
I believe women,
First before all, should be
Enshrined as
Gods
"The gift to
All"

Money and Power

Remember lost souls
Who you truly are,
For if you pretend,
You will exist in life
In the shadow of
Hell
This I grieve, you
Will always regret
Your obsession for the money and
Power we chase
Rewards us with lives of
Disgrace and empty
Space
And when our time is due
And there is no one with you,
Remember it was
No one but you,
Who did not prevail
And let your life fail

Pride

Be forewarned for
Now I speak
Heed the words your
Ears will hear
Be not ashamed of your
Station or color
Or to whom you were born
Stand high atop the
Mountain
Open thy heart and
Bellow these
Words of truth
"It is I, I am proud"
From whence I came
For I carry
My family name

The Headless Horseman Rides Again

The rumor spread all over town on what might
Happen at midnight Halloween
1930
Excitement and fright surround the
Town folks
For they were told the "Headless
Horseman" would rise from
The dead and ride
Again
Suddenly the sky turned eerie
Black
Time was here, one shadow
Circled the old horse
Stable
A black horse he wanted to
Match the night
He swore an oath to the full
Moon
"I will ride to the
Center of town and back
This Halloween"
Horse saddled, costume on,
The clock strikes midnight
The ride is on
The Horseman galloped
Down Main St.
Lantern blazing, he screamed like a
Banshee
Children and grown-ups alike, out
For candy, run crying with fright
"The Headless Horseman is back from the
dead
God save us on this night"

With the thunder of hooves and
Lantern blazing bright, the Horseman entered
The center of town
The curious and nonbelievers run
Drenched in fear
Horse covered with sweat and breathing fire
The Horseman circled around for
The second time
Sirens blazed red and blue,
Lights flashing, the police
Arrived
But the "Headless Horseman"
Not impressed circled again
So he would have no regrets
Not afraid of any human
For on this day, he rose from
The dead
He was gloating on this
Resurrected night
Of hell
Leaving the police and everyone gasping
With fear, praying
The "Headless Horseman"
Would never appear
Again
He disappeared into the
Black night
Screaming this chilling promise . . .
"I, the Headless Horseman,
Will rise from the dead and ride
Amongst you
Again"
To this day, all
Wonder
Was that true
If so,

When then will the
"Headless Horseman"
Bare his soul
And appear again
As she crumbled the
Morning newspaper in her hand
Mom said, "never your
Dad
Has taken his last Halloween ride

The Love of Ravioli

Sixth grade, ten years old
St. Mary's School, to the grotto restaurant
Wednesdays,
They march like Roman soldiers down Scovill Street
Dreaming of being served like the nobles were
Today's special, the waiter proclaimed
A dish of "4 ravioli and a glass of coke" .35 cents
Pockets emptied quickly, they spoke out boldly
"We will all have a dish of 4 and a glass"
Not having .35 cents but a lot of moxie,
Young Dino held the door with his left hand as people exited
And like a fox, held out his right hand for a tip,
Quickly earning .35 cents
He then ran in, joined his friends, and shouted
"Me too, 4 and a glass, please!"

The Soldier's War Prayer

I wonder alone and
Afraid
Except for death which accompanies
Me
In the midst of confusion and despair
I pray as does everyone to
Their God
But
If God is the same to all
Which God
Will answer
When we all ask in prayer
"Dear God
Let me live"
Shall it be the enemy
Or me
Choose one side or the other
Lord
Am I the enemy or is
He
In the eyes of thee
I beg no one knows
For many die and many
Live
Tell me, dear Lord,
How will you decide
Will it be I who
Survives

The Prom

She entered the room reminiscent of
A sweet summer breeze
Hair perfect glistening in
The brightly lit lights
She knows all eyes are on her
Flicks her head and nods
Acknowledgement
Breathtaking, how does one
Describe perfection
Agreed, absolutely nothing
Of her needed correction
People inched closer to her
Ignoring who they were
With
My God, what a body, legs
To the sky, eyes like stars,
Makeup flawless,
She's mine
Perfect in every respect
Compared to other women
In attendance
No contest
How does one describe
Perfection
She is a queen of the prom
Such beauty
A pleasure to be seen
We woke in the morning, her
Words I will never
Forget,
"Take me again, my
King"

Where Do Angels Come From

Christmas masses thankfully over,
Time for going home to Christmas dinner
Francisco, St. Michael's head
Altar boy yawns
The deluxe altar chair looks
Especially inviting today
He sits, closes his eyes, and
Wanders off into the
Spiritual world
Francisco decides to ask the same
Question again he has always asked
Especially on Christmas
"Lord, ten years I have served
Mass, four alone this Christmas day,
Your humble servant begs
For this answer
Where do angels come from?"
Instantly, there appeared the
Most beautiful light
Embracing the entire altar, glorious
Shades of blue, gold, purple,
And white
Dancing softly to the haunting sound
Of heavenly
Music
Blessing each object on the
Altar as it touched them
Ever so
Reverently
Francisco retreated deeper into
Sleep
A hypnotic voice lovingly
Speaks,

"Sin and evil have soiled
This world
Great sorrow and pain does
The Lord God feels
Our Lord God absorbs those
Sin and evil deeds unto
Himself
Again saving mankind over
And over again"
Thou, my Lord, is almighty
Above all
Such great sorrow his heart
Feels, that miraculously
A holy tear he does
Shed
"Francisco, my child, that tear
Becomes an angel
So now you know
Where angels come from"
Francisco never arrived home
For Christmas dinner
His family and Father John
Found him lying at the angel's
Monument
As
St. Michael carried Francisco
To his true home
Where Jesus welcomed
Him to heaven for an
Angel he had
Become

Dreams within a Dream

Dedicated to the memory of Frank McCourt.

RAY SPRINGER

A Little Life–Time in a Day

When you think about it,
each day is like a
little life-time;
With the rising Sun
The day is born;
Then a little work,
A little play-
Some tears perhaps,
Some laughter, and time
Erases all thereafter!
The Earth keeps turning,
Clocks keep ticking away-
All inevitable…
As we wind our way
'til the end of the day.
Soon back to sleep again.
Ah! Is there anything better?
Night brings rest…
We close our tired eyes
Stars and dreams
Come on as our little
Day is done. Morning,
Noon, Evening and Night-
A little life-time
Has had its run.
Another day has come
And gone, slipped
Through the fingers of
Time forever, forever!

Chess and Life

Life is much like a game of Chess;
One must strive to make the right moves,
And, conversely, foolish moves are costly.
One must know when
To sacrifice for the greater good.
Life itself is King
And must be protected at all times.
One must stay alert and be ready,
While at the same time
Casting an eye down the future,
And thinking at least a few moves ahead.

7A.M. Express

Sardines with sleepy faces
Packed in a rolling machine
Travel toward their paychecks
A weary discipline.
Some sad, some intelligent faces
Lulled and dulled
By a motor's drab drone;
Most faces expressing
The wish that this were instead
The journey returning home!

Forest Mysticism

There is a church in an autumnal forest;
And a benevolence in solitude and silence.
A mystic presence permeates the atmosphere;
No human sounds are wanted or needed;
No human chaos and confusion here.

One finds music in a rolling stream and
Peace in the chirping of a solitary bird–
Natural melodies that soothe the soul.

Hence the spirit, absorbed in wonder and awe,
Is assuaged by a wordless-healing quiet.
Only the wind seems to whisper-
"Ah! Here every day is a holy day!"

Karma

Look behind you, friend.
Across the sands of time…
Your footsteps always follow,
For wherever we go
We leave traces behind
Never to be erased.
Just as the Moon
Can never cease to effect
The ever-pliant seas,
Or the Earth can ever run
From the pull of the Sun,
We can never escape
The trail we leave behind us.
So look behind you, friend,
And ask yourself:
Are you happy with
The life path you are taking?

Like Books?

Our lives are like books;
Our days like pages;
Our years like chapters.
Each life a story in time
With beginning,
Middle and end.
We live out our plots
With the Almighty, The
Omniscient Author, Who
Determines the lengths!

Mystic Union

When the sponge is in the water,
The water is in the sponge.
When a person is in love,
Love is in the person.
When we live in truth,
Truth follows in our actions.
When we live with awareness
Of God's presence, God's
Spirit lives in us!

Never Compare Love

Never compare love to a rose.
For though a flower is beautiful
It lives but for a season,
And love should last forever!
Neither compare love to a star,
For though a star's light is great,
Time will diminish its intensity,
And love should be immune to time!
Neither compare love to the sea,
For though the sea has immensity,
There is an end to water at last,
And love should be boundless!
Love can't be compared at all!
It is a matter quite unique,
Timeless, omnipotent and boundless,
Having no Earthly comparison!

No Taxes or Inflation

No taxes or inflation
Can mar the sparkling stars;
These gems are freely ours!

No tariff can ever
Diminish the Sun in
All its beauty.
Its glory is ours
Free of duty!

Like love that has
No price, and friendship
Which seeks no fee,
Most precious things
In life are free,
And shall forever be!

Bee-ing Busy

Observe the busy, buzzing bee
So diligent in its flight. It
Has no need for watches or clocks–
It hasn't got the time.
It has an important task to do,
And flies right to it
And does a honey of a job
Making our world a sweeter place!

Peace of Mind

When Peace rests in a quiet mind,
A gem like this cannot be bought.
Greater comfort one cannot find.
What gold can purchase serene thought?
What more precious can ever be
Than a mind that is trouble free?
Seek not gold, fame or lover's stare,
Nor power or ambition chase
For there is nothing here but care,
These will not lead the mind to ease.
What is kinder in life to find
Than the joy of a tranquil mind?

Space, Time and Mind

What portion of space we own
We learn from studying Astronomy.
How little time we are here
We learn from studying History.
How much to us is yet unknown
We learn from great Philosophy.
In learning from these three
We build a needed immunity
To the folly of human vanity!

The Bank OF Life

If one makes no deposit
In the Bank of life,
One has no right to complain
When there is nothing to withdraw,
For, obviously, one is living
Life without interest!

A Prayer for Peace

Lord, bring us
Peace this day,
That we may
Be helpful and kind
To all our brothers
And sisters.
For we—the family of Man,
Are all children
Of one Almighty God!
Though Your Absolute Will
Is inscrutable,
These things we feel,
Dear Lord, are true:
Our first duty
In life itself is
That we love one another
—and that love is
Your Divine Will!
Let this Will dwell
In every heart and
That all war end
Upon the Earth forever
Amen!

To the Country of the Mind

Now the city has
It's amenities,
to this I would
certainly agree;
Yet there are times
On days
When all the noise
And chaos
Can really get to a person.
On such days seek quiet
Contemplation.
One must ensconce
Oneself snuggly
In the salubrious
Contentment
That comes with silence
And solitude.
Find a place blessed
with seclusion
where the mind
can soothe itself
with such simple
remedies as
reading a story,
or a poem.
Or escape to far
Away lands,
Vicariously visiting
Another time
Across the pages
Of a masterpiece.
Or retreat into a world
Of meditation.

Ah yes! When city
Pace and hassle
Frazzle that last nerve,
quickly, quickly!
Travel to the country
Of the mind…

The Golden Path

The Bird of moderation
Never flies too far–
Experience has taught him
Just where his limits are.

Since all things share proportion,
Carry few things to excess,
For the path of moderation
Most often leads to success.

So try not to overdo it–
All things having clear limits,
The reasonable path is best.
One who lives with moderation
Will live a life that's blest!

The Three Ships of Time

Yesterday has sailed–
A ship out of sight!
Tomorrow is a cargo
That may never reach port!
Today alone is docked
And waits to be unloaded,
But do not tarry, my friends,
Her anchorage is short!

Treasures for the Soul

Now many value strings of pearl,
Quite naturally and well, but not I.
You see, I see my true love's smile,
And it is a true treasure for my soul.
Oh! The world still covets chunks of gold,
And this too is simple to understand,
But I am happy my love's hand to hold;
This also is a treasure for my soul.
Search all you want for red, red rubies,
Of such desires I am entirely free,
For my love's eyes are sparkling stars
Beaming their light of love to me.
No! I do not value such worldly toys
Mere paltry trinkets for fools to see.
When two share love's mystic joys,
What more precious in life can there be?

Unconditional Love

Brandy, you're a good dog,
What a good pal you have been!
You're a loyal, good-natured fellow
Without a touch of human sin.
Never once have you cared
About what I possess.
Never have you thought me
A failure or success.
In the race of human life
Petting you has given me rest;
And in your devoted eyes,
As well as in your thumping breast,
I sense an unconditional love
That few, if any, human can attest.
Brandy, you're such a good dog!

Zen And Now

Nothing remains…,
Everything is on its way from here to there,
And even before it arrives,
It plans to be somewhere else.
A child grabs a handful of water
Only to realize that it can't be held.
It vanishes before the hand is opened,
Even less substantial than smoke in the wind.
Now is an infinitesimal island
In an endless ocean of infinite time;
A momentary perception
That has the veracity of a dream.

Poetic Justice

To the Good Lord above,
You taught me so much with unconditional Love.
You're more than just my Father, indeed you are my friend.
Thank you for never leaving me, I love you God…
Amen!

SPARKLE KENNER

To My Father Floyd with Love and Memories

You're all that a father could and should be
As a little girl you were and still are my hero
Your tolerance level for ignorance was zero
You are so intelligent and so very wise
I was daddy's little girl and that's no lie
When you were away from home I would not clean my room
Until mommy said she'd take pictures and send them to you
I still smile when I think of how you showed your stash to me
You hid your money in the angel on top of the Christmas tree
We used to have family time and play board games
And when I had my own children I showed them the same
I love being your daughter I'm so proud you're my dad
You've held my hand through good times and even the bad
You taught me the difference between right and wrong
And through all the trials and tribulations you always stayed strong
So many good qualities I possess because of you
I know you love me daddy and I really love you too

A Lost Love

So we meet up again after all these years, memories come flooding followed by tears. Knowing what I know now I can honestly say, that I lost a part of me every time you went away. Remember that day in the city we danced and sang? Every single word to "you are my everything". That's how I felt I was nothing without you, so when you got locked up I did not know what else to do. I began to turn to drugs thinking that would ease the pain, of losing the only man I loved, my thinking was insane. As the years go by I'm still sitting here trying to make it right, my days are spent working hard and alone in bed at night. I must admit lately that I've been playing a little pretend, telling myself that we're together and back in love again. You're so genuine and that's why I love you so very much. It only takes your voice, you don't even have to touch. All you have to do is simply say "peace", and somehow you completely put my weary soul at ease. So many tears and sad ones too, reminiscing on the past and the hurt I caused you. So young and naive I wish I knew better, I wish I didn't have to talk through these letters. I really want to see you and look at your face, giving you up was my biggest mistake. Now married again and you have a new son, but for thirteen years I was the one. What can I do to make things right? I kiss your picture before I sleep at night. When I finally saw you after nine long years, I tried really hard to fight back the tears. I asked how do I start to try to make amends? You simply replied, "try being my friend." This may be the hardest thing I've ever done, saying goodbye to the only man that I've loved. I promise I will try with all of my might, to let go of the past and respect your new wife…

A Poem for My Beautiful Baby Girl Donesha Jasmine Kenner

I'm sitting in a jail cell barely keeping my head above water
When a quiet voice whispers to me "go ahead and write your daughter"
I tell you Donesha, I still remember the beautiful day you were born.
It was cold outside, I was ready to go, and your father helped me along.
The pain was crazy I started to wonder if you could feel my reactions
Your dad called the cab and while we waited we tried to time contractions.
We made it to the hospital room it was packed with family and friends
But the doctor said there was no way that everybody could stay in
I chose my cousin Stacy my mom and of course your dad
Everyone was filled with joy and I have never been so glad
Finally, the day had come for us our beautiful blessing arrived
I looked down and saw my own reflection through my daughter's eyes Through the years at times I was scared and did not know what to do
All I know is I wanted to be the best mother I could for you
I made mistakes and caused you pain it was those times I wanted to die
But I promised myself no matter what for you I'd stay alive
My eyes are filling with tears even as I write this poem
Because I know somewhere you are waiting for me to come on home
Just do me one favor and say your prayers whenever you lay in your bed
Because I honestly believe when I talk to God he will tell me what you said
At least the things you say to Him that you really want me to know
Like you love me so much no matter what and you need me to stay at home
Hopefully you can quiet your thoughts and see what God can do
Lately I've been asking Him to please tell you I miss and love you too

Always

Always be encouraged at the end of the day,
And never give up hope, everything will be okay.
Always keep praying for things to turn out right
And never forget to thank him each and every night.
Always read your Bible and trust in Him above
1st Corinthians chapter 13 is all about His love.
Always remember to love others as much as you love yourself
And never turn a blind eye when someone seeks your help.
Don't get so caught up in this life that you begin to ignore the truth
That no matter how rough it seems to be, Angels still are watching you.
Keep in mind whatever you do its progress not perfection.
Our heavenly father knows our hearts and all our good intentions
Never think for a minute that you alone have troubles
Thank you, Lord, because of you, were stronger from our struggles.

Children Lost to Drugs

I never imagined it would hurt this bad.
I miss my children and I feel real sad.
The most physical pain was the day they were born
And the most heartache I felt was the day they were gone.
Even with childbirth, I still felt pleasure
And when I look in their eyes nothing else could measure.
I know there is nothing in this world I won't do.
It was them that made me happy whenever I felt blue.
How could I have messed up these blessings so bad?
So many bad choices really making me mad.
I know I was young, and did not know much better
I break down and cry and then pull it together.
I feel like I failed them, what more can I say?
I wonder will the guilt and shame ever go away.
I love my children, they remind me of myself.
All I really needed was some genuine help.
Instead of people so quick to take them from me
Couldn't anyone teach me, to be the best mom I could be?
Even now as I sit here in this cell crying
I remember when I lost them and how I felt like dyeing.
I started turning to drugs just to ease the pain
Marijuana and PCP I was smoking every day.
It was the only time in my life I began to ask God why
I felt like when I lost them a part of me died.
I stayed hopeful and strong and one day they came home
It was good for a while and then something went wrong.
After a few good years I felt myself start to fall
If I could turn back time, I would have never made that call.
PCP is a drug that can make you lose your mind
so I took the risk of smoking and lost them a second time.
I pray all the time that it's not too late.
That God once again will make for us a way.
Only He knows how I feel deep down inside

And only He can determine if I get another try.
In God and only God do I put all of my trust
And never again no matter what will I ever turn to drugs
I can hear God telling me "always protect your mind."
And so much more will be revealed through the course of time.
Crying makes me tired so it's time to go to sleep
This is my cry until the next time this pen and paper meet.

Conscious

How dare you keep going like everything's alright?
Like I ain't see you rape that little girl last night.
I watched how you beat her and slapped her in the face
I've been a witness your whole life, you've been such a disgrace.
I bet that you did not think that anyone ever saw
Those times you drank, pissed yourself and passed out on the floor.
You call women bitches like it makes you bigger
And behind closed doors you call people niggers.
You robbed an old lady and stole from your mom.
Remember that time you tried to build a bomb?
These things you thought that no one would find out
I stayed real quiet but now I'm about to shout.
Oh, that's real tough look at you pulling out your gun,
Well unlike everyone else I'm not going to run
Go ahead and shoot, add to your nonsense
I can't die partner…Cause I'm your conscious.

Drug of Choice

Hey, you, can I get a minute? Don't you recognize my voice?
I know you ain't forget about me, I'm your drug of choice.
After everything we been through, come on let's not pretend
If I remember clearly, we use to be best friends.
For me you would of did anything and now you claim it's over
Look at you really feeling yourself because you're clean and sober
You use to love me and no matter what, you'd always put me first
And every time you called on me I was there to quench your thirst
You told me nobody would listen and only I understood your pain
Now you think you can make it without me? That sounds real insane.
I see you getting your life together and starting to look real strong
Some say you're better off without me but we both know that their wrong
See death do us part that was and still continues to be my motto
So it's okay if I don't see you today, I'll catch up with you tomorrow.
I saw you last night, crying in your room claiming to hate my guts
Blaming me, saying it's my fault that your life got all messed up.
I could not help but laugh because you act as if you can't see
That you were the one who always came, running right back to me.
So at the end of the day the choice is yours, you can leave me and go do better
Just remember when you contact me I warned you in this letter.
I'm mad that you found the secret to keeping me out your life
The stunt this time you pulled on me it cut just like a knife
I feel like you betrayed me when you finally found your voice
And you prayed to God the only one stronger than me,
Sincerely,
Your drug of choice

Exercise

On my way to the gym, it's time to get in shape.
It's not good to live your life and in society overweight.
It's not that I'm insecure about what people may say
Because it's really not about them I just want to live today.
Good health is just one of the things I always took for granted
But when I finally went to the doctor's right then the seed was planted.
Arthritis in my knee I'm not getting any younger
Time to change my eating habits to satisfy my hunger.
I have got to do better, ya know drink lots of water
Today I decided to exercise and get my life in order.

His Hand

Because His hand is on me, I am still alive
Because His hand is on me, I know I will survive.
When I stop to think about, the kind of life I lived,
I say, "Thank you Heavenly Father" because I know that you forgive.
My poor choices have gotten me in a world of trouble
But you kept your hand on me throughout all my struggles.
With His hand He lets me know just how much I'm worth it.
With his hands he molded me and shaped me to be perfect.
With his hands he's managed to always keep me close.
He was always there for me at times I did not know.
Now that I am older, I finally understand
Our awesome God really has the whole world in His hands.

Lord Calling

What will I be when I grow up?
The coffee was done so I poured a cup.
I thought maybe a doctor, or I'd love to sing
Or maybe I'll get married with a big wedding ring.
As the years passed by, I felt my dreams falling
I was in a jail cell when I realized my calling.
I'm going to teach the youth about Jesus Christ
How He loved the world so much that He gave up His life.
How many of us would get on a cross?
Be beaten and ridiculed? I cringe at the thought.
Thank you Lord you did that for us
I never knew that you cared so much.
Teach me how to love like you
Where do I start? And what do I do?
It starts with me that's what you say
I have to have something to give away
Like knowledge, wisdom and understanding
to share with the world without being demanding?
It sounds pretty easy "Do you think I can?"
He said, "together absolutely" and held my hand.

Love

Somebody asked the question: what is this thing called Love?
So I referred the question to the good Lord up above.
He said Love is patient and love it is so kind
Love is those who stand by your side till the end of time.
I said I want to tell everyone about how he loves me most
He shook his head and simply said "real Love it doesn't boast!"
Then He said there's something else that you need to know:
Love keeps no record of wrongdoings or says I told you so
Love is nothing like evil and very slow to anger
Love is a safe haven that keeps you out of danger.
As His voice starts to fade, I think of his words and look around this jail
I notice my Bible is open to 1st Corinthians 13 about Love… It never fails!

Married

I am single, but you are not
So all this flirting has to stop
You can say what you want to say about me
But please respect my recovery.
I'm making changes and you are one
I am no longer having "sex for fun."
You have a wife and many problems
Stop looking at me to help you solve them.
I'm not saying don't live your life
All I'm saying is respect your wife
And respect me enough to let it go
My yes meant yes but now my no means no.
I really need you to give me some space
My emotions got involved and it won't be the same
I don't know what I was thinking, you're a married man
You may not agree but I hope you understand.
The relationship we had, took me for a toll.
When we got intimate I lost all control.
No more moving backwards, I'm only moving on
Concentrating on loving me and giving it to God.

My First Grandbaby

Looking into my grandson's eyes, I'm filled with joy and so much pride. You give me a purpose baby Akeem, a reason to Hope a reason to dream. As I listen to your tiny cries I just want to keep you by my side. I never knew a love so sweet I count ten little toes on your very little feet. I would talk to you even before you were born, and I prayed for your arrival into this world. I'm so blessed to be able to hold you now you're my first and only baby grandchild.

New Baby

There's something I need to tell you, that's heavy on my mind
I been searching for the words to say and asking for a sign
I'm not sure if you will be happy, I just know it's overdue
Sit down please; relax your mind while I attempt to explain to you
It's more than how you kiss me; maybe it's how you hold me tight
That makes me know I have to tell you because it's only right.
When you respond just be gentle and remember I'm still your lady
What I have to say is congratulations we're going to have a baby.

Peace

Why does it seem like nobody wants me around?
I keep hoping one day, again I'll be found.
Once I was so wanted that people fought for me
Who am I you ask? My name is PEACE.
I'm not down for fighting, not even for a cause
My favorite line of question is "Can't we all get along?"
Controversy seems to be everywhere I go
I try to intercede, and some tell me no.
Since when did drama become so great?
And since when did killing someone become their own fate?
Don't you know there is karma and it can happen to you?
Kill someone for wearing red then you die wearing blue.
This vicious cycle, when will it end?
Stop being enemy's and start to be friends.
War is not the solution nor is it the answer.
It's pointless and kills. Something like cancer.
It's time to get together and seek "the big guy upstairs"
So why not join together and talk to him in prayer?
Ask Him to please put our minds at ease
And fill us with the gentle spirit of kindness, love and peace.

Poetic Justice

It's really okay, call it what you may
Poetic justice is what I say.
It's a form of expressing pleasure and pain,
Seeking out justice and not only blame.
Some say that my poetry makes them feel good
Others say it helps them think out of the hood.
In all of my poems I strive to see
Identification and unity.
I write about God because all props to Him.
He is our maker and forgiver of sins.
So much injustice remains in this world
Love for one another is what we need more.
As a people we must start to ask ourselves
What can we do to heal and help?
A friendly word can go such a long way
And a smile can really brighten one's day.
When was the last time you helped a stranger?
Was I the only one God kept you out of danger?
I urge everyone, before it is too late,
To not only please God but get to the gate
When it's all over and everything said and done,
Did you really make a difference or were you busy having fun?

Pray Worries Away

So many times, I want to cry,
For no reason at all I don't know why.
There are days that are better than others
Then some days I just feel smothered.
I'm so overcome with regret and shame
When I start thinking about mistakes I've made,
Then I pray to God to help me feel better
And sometimes I write a gratitude letter.
I remember reading some time ago
You can't be depressed AND thankful so…
I write a list of all my blessings
And before you know it, I'm no longer stressing.
I'm alive and well and that's just a start
And I have a God who knows my heart.
So any bad feelings, I shake them off
And demand the enemy to go get lost.
Because I am happy, the Lord and me
He dries my tears, so I can see,
That this person that I came to be
My God He loves me unconditionally.
So whenever I have doubts and start feeling down
I just pray until things turn around.
Thank you, God, for what you do
All of my faith is always in you.

Released

In a few hours I'm going home
And thank you God, I won't be alone.
Everywhere I go, I know can turn to you
I stay prayed up for those confused.
Sitting in jail, letting time pass by
Never once acknowledging you're by their side
Don't they know that you can do anything?
Or all about the joy and peace you bring.
If only they would learn just how to let go
And be more trusting that you're in control
I spent the past eight months getting myself together
Realizing that you love me always and forever
All of the years I sped through life
You waited patiently for me to get it right.
When you saw where I was heading, you said "that's enough"
You took me from the streets and away from the drugs.
At times I was sad and even shed some tears
But you stayed by my side and showed that you care.
I love you Lord and cannot even say
How much I appreciate waking up today.
Thank you for showing me how special I am
Jeremiah 29:11 talking about your plans.
Everything I do, I will try to do your speed
So when they open up these prison doors please continue guiding me.

I Come First

Do you know what it's like to do too much?
When your head is just clouded with lots of "stuff."
To take on people's problems like there your own
When you don't even have a place to call home.
It's not a game, I'm not at all playing
Please don't confuse what I am saying.
I want to ask a question hypothetically
How can I love you and not lose me?
Giving so much of myself
Running around trying to help, help, help.
Never slowing down to take care of me
What about the goals I'd like to achieve?
Now I know for better or worst
It's a must I put myself first.
Once I sought out the Lord in prayer
Suddenly the answers were clear
How can I help other's if I'm not okay?
I have to come first starting today
All of the sudden I really understand
Until I love myself, I can't love a man.

Love Inside

I don't know how to tell you no.
I want so bad to take things slow
It's like you're forcing me to stay
and you refuse to let me walk away.
Why can't you understand, this is not the time?
I have too many other things on my mind
but I just don't want to see you sad
and if I tell you how I feel your mad
it has nothing to do with you as a man.
Pease read these words and try to understand.
I have some work to do on myself,
and it requires the Good Lord's help.
I need to know how to love again
So, I asked Allah what is the plan.
I deserve to be loved and put myself
first before the day comes that I'm up in a hearse.
I don't want to keep going in circles
feeling too weak to overcome hurdles.
Life is full of ups and downs, it's
time 2 face them with no one around.
Insha Allah I'll get better with me
and then I can really love somebody
no more relationships, now's just not the time
I'm so thankful for the strength to love me inside.

New Year's

It's a new year with a brand-new start,
time to make changes that's good for the heart.
Let it all go after we reflect on the past
time to look forward without moving too fast.
The new year is the perfect time to spread
happiness and always be kind.
So, toast to good changes that start within you.
Make resolutions of things to change
and work on them a little each day.
We all know Rome was not built overnight.
So, don't get crazy. Keep your goals in sight,
and if you start slacking dust yourself off,
straighten out your crown and be your own boss.
Be responsible of all the changes you make, give
more of yourself, and be slower to take some loved
ones did not make it this year.
So, thank our higher power that we are still here,
remember that actions speak louder than words,
so, this new year let's SHOW Him he's first.

Test of Faith

Why do I feel so all alone?
No matter where I'm at or where I go.
I feel unloved and I don't know why.
I can have dozens of people by my side still I feel like nobody cares.
I'm trying to shake the feeling that I need someone here.
I know that it's best for it to be this way,
I might cry tonight but tomorrow's a new day.
I have a history of overextending myself I can love you
and lose me so I sought out some help.
Jehovah told me that love comes from within.
To just hold on and be my own friend.
He said don't let a man become your idol
I'm everything you need so look to me child
only I will love you with unconditional love
stop hurting yourself with all of these drugs
do something different to help ease the pain
there would be no rainbow if it wasn't for rain.
Now put the pen down and get you some rest,
you were never alone this was only a test.

Thank You

There is no way in this world, I can thank you enough
For everything you do for me, it's just so very much.
Thank you for the very air that I need to breathe
And thank you for all the goals you helped me to achieve.
I still thank you for down times, because they helped me grow
And when I was wrong, thank you for not saying: "I told you so."
Thank you for loving me like nobody else does,
And thank you for blessing me with my daughter and my son.
Thank you, Lord, for never ever giving up on me
And thank you for being my eyes when I could not see.
Thank you for my parents, who both are still alive,
And thank you God for saving me at times I could have died.
I really appreciate how much you really care.
And thank you Jesus for telling me, to never live in fear.
I could go on forever just simply thanking you
I love you God and appreciate everything you do.

To my son Donovan

Feeling alone and pregnant, not sure of what to do
About to have a baby that's one thing that I knew.
Right from the beginning the doctor said you'd be a boy
In a cold world full of misery, I knew you'd be my joy.
Right from the start during labor we ran into some trouble
Umbilical cord wrapped around your neck as you began to struggle.
I started to cry and pray to god "Please let my baby be safe."
And before I knew it I was staring down as your handsome little face.
The years passed by and I still remember like it was yesterday
7/14 that's my birthday, and just how much you weighed.
I swear baby boy I really did try, to be the best mom I could be
I made mistakes and many nights I cried myself to sleep.
The should've, could've, and would've's always sneak into my head
I start to miss you even more and regret the things not said
You're such a big part of my life, more than just my son
All the nights I wanted to give up you're the reason I dropped the gun.
When the reality hits me, of how I failed you it's hard for me to breathe
Even as I put these words together sadness starts taking over me.
Its times like this and many more I have to give to God
Ask Him to forgive my sins and make me a better mom.
I pray and have faith that no matter what we will be together soon
At home just chilling, chopping it up, or even in the booth.
Whatever dreams and goals you have with God they will come true
Just remember no matter where you go, your mom is going too.

You Are Always by My Side and Thankful for That

You are always by my side and thankful for that
Weather I am reading, writing or just kicking back.
When I open up the Bible sometimes it really says
Exactly what it is, I'm thinking in my head.
I know that I must work on gaining self-control
You're watching all my actions this is something that I know.
It is you heavenly Father who knows me in and out
You fill me with confidence and never with self-doubt.
It's because of you that most days are filled with laughter
I have faith in your promise of a happily ever after.
There is no hiding from you because I know you see it all
And although at times I stumble, I will never fall.
With your blessings I know that I can do anything
It's like were married and your Love is our wedding ring.
You give hearing to the death and vision for blind to see
I love being a part of you, and you a part of me.
Every day I am reminded that the choice is mine
With my body locked in jail, I still can free my mind.
As I look at the women around me I realize I've been saved
Some of us came very close to lying in our graves.
It's good to use time wisely and start to understand,
That destroying our lives in anyway was never in Gods plans.
Once we start to know how beautiful we are inside
The pain will start to go away and fears they will subside
When we know our capability then sky is the very limit
And we play the game of life constantly to win it.
We should always keep in mind whenever the road is rough
That it is written three things remain that's our faith, our hope, and love.

I'm Blessed

When I think of all the thing's
The Good Lord's done for me
*I know I'm Blessed
When I remember where I been
And how He allowed me to live again
*I know I'm Blessed
When I get sad and start to sigh
There's no need to wonder why
When nothing seems to go right
And I'm crying every night
*Still I know I'm Blessed
Nothing at all can shake my faith
Didn't He wake me up today?
*Oh yes, I'm Blessed
Sometimes I smile, sometimes I frown
I remain optimistic even when I feel down
*Because I'm Blessed
So what if I lost my phone
Some people don't have a home
*Of course, I'm Blessed
We have to open our hearts and see
How much He cares for you and me
*You know we're Blessed
So when the day's keep getting longer
And your wishing you were stronger
Go somewhere quiet and stop the stressing
Wait on Him and receive your Blessings.

Crossroads

How did I get here? That's the question of the day.
I'm at a crossroad in my life and I don't know what to say.
To the left is surely heartache and pain
And to the right is promises of a brighter day
To the right there are thing's much better for me
Like saying no to drugs and yes to sobriety
To the right there is promises of a new way to live
I heard the people there have lots of love to give
To the left is the road I'm more familiar with
A bunch of thing's I'm scared I'll miss
Like doing what I want and saying how I feel
You might call me crazy but I'm just keeping it real
Now I'm standing at this crossroad still trying with all my might
Out of habit I step to the left, but something pulls me right
So here it is I'm stepping out solely based on faith
Because I'm ready to live life RIGHT starting here today.

Prison Life

Who needs a TV with all the drama I see
Confused inmates thinking they're the police
If you can't take jail, stop committing crimes
Sick of all the complaining, sick of all the lies
Talking about it's not your fault and how somebody did you wrong
Then there's those who make it home but don't last for very long
Today an officer told me "this place is a revolving door "
I rolled my eyes, shook my head and then looked down at the floor
It's really sad and crazy to see
How comfortable jails starting to be
Three hots and a cot is what my pops use to say
At least that's what they called it back in the day
Ain't no law library or going to school
Instead they wheel in a computer we don't know how to use
The girl in the next cell keeps screaming out her door
Trying to get the nurse's attention all I hear is "give me more"
She's fresh off the streets still trying to get high
A few more cells down a girl committed suicide
Somebody should have warned her you have to pay to play
And we all have to answer to a higher power on judgement day
All of these things going down right inside my mind
As I lay in my cell praying that this will be the final time.

Old Friend

After all this time I ain't expect to see you
Walk over to me in the visiting room
Never thought once again I'd be looking in your eyes
I must admit old friend this is such a pleasant surprise
What I cherish the most is we both think alike
Both playing it cool trying to do this thing right
We've been through a lot and really hurt each other
Sometimes we were friends other times we were lovers
One thing I really feel obligated to say
I miss your friendship at the end of the day
The same way you're feeling, I feel about you
You're changing for the better I'm so proud of you boo
It was nice to conversate and express how we feel
I love how no matter what you always stayed real
We both are grown and have no reason to lie
I know that another girl left you hurting inside
I can't say that I can make everything better
But I did pour my heart out in a seven-page letter
So there you have it and I wrote you this poem
And that's just to hold you until I get home
Maybe one day we can try "us" again
Either way it was nice to see you my friend.

Corrupted System

They lock away our people and throw away the key
Lord what must we do to set our families free?
Locked up behind bars like animals in a cage Tempers building up subjected to so much pain
If you have a lot of money you can make it out of court
The system is so corrupted where is the support?
My only son is locked up for basically stealing
When the judge sentenced him, there was no concealing
All the pain, the confusion and the tears
Yes, it was wrong, but they gave him twelve years
What would you do if it was your child
Stand up for justice or be in denial?
My best friend is locked up for self-defense
Legal corruption it just doesn't make sense
Sitting under the sign that says in God we trust
The lack of True Justice is really disgusting
I will stay in prayer and try to remain humble
Till the day our Lord comes and the courtrooms all crumble
then the person in the robe really will see
Who is the ONLY righteous judge of you and of me

The War Within

Galatians 5:17
Speaks of a war between
The spirit and flesh
And how we must choose best
The spirit produces thing's such as kindness and love
While the flesh likes fighting, idolatry and drugs
Who wins the fight that goes on within ourselves?
The side that will win will be the side that we help.

A Mother's Love

This poem is dedicated to my mother.
Oh, how I love you, I remember the struggle. Thinking back to when I was just a child,
And how many times she went the extra mile.
We never had to worry about food to eat
She worked two jobs to earn her keep.
She put up with abuse and Daddy's addiction Her children's happiness was her everyday mission.
She taught us good morals and all about respect
She did everything she could to keep our family in check.
To this day mom you are my rock
and my love for you will never stop.
I can only keep trying, hope and pray
To be half the mother you are to my children someday.

The Resolution

Life is a struggle and that is so real.
Keep pressing on beyond how you feel.
As far as I can remember, I keep me a job
No credit it to me, always Alhamdulillah.
I'm all grown up now, had to cease these silly stunts.
No more wasting life on drugs and smoking blunts.
I rid myself of toxic things full of evil and pollution
Wondering why people still ask, "where's the resolution?"
Everyone may not always respect a person's heart
So be wise about the company you keep, that play's a major part.
The best thing for someone else may not always be best for you
We were all created different and unique this much I know is true.
The bottom line is try digging inside
Always be humble never deal in false pride
Find your passion and make it your purpose
Live a productive life cause trust me your worth it.

Forever Love

I fell apart,
when I lost my heart
I cried a million billion tears
And said a trillion zillion prayers.
It was my fault you went away,
My mouth said go but my soul said stay.
Once you vanished, so did I
I fell real hard, I lost my mind.
It took some years, but I got back up
I prayed for help to stop the drugs.
Now I know I will and can
Start to heal and love again
There's just one problem with moving on
We still have this love and unbreakable bond
It's complicated now you're with someone new
But you still love me, and I love you too
I'm not sure I can be your second wife
When I put you first all of my life
I'll stay in prayer and ask for strength
To never again make the same mistakes
I'll keep Allah first, He surely knows best
Cause If loving you Is wrong…well you know the rest.
I'm finally convinced, we don't need no closure
cause this "forever love" we share will never be over.

More Than Words

Remember when marriage was the number one goal?
And now it's a struggle just staying faithful.
Even when your woman is loving you right,
Or your man work's hard and comes home every night
As humans we want the things we can't have
We say we want good but gravitate towards the bad
It used to be simple, this thing called love
Rare and beautiful like watching a dove
When did love turn into confusion and pain?
And since when did love leave you out in the rain?
It's simple to say those three little words,
Especially when you're feeling the love in return.
To love someone with no conditions
It's always easier said than done
If you love somebody, then treat them right
Don't hurt them or look for reasons to fight
Never lose your love because a distraction
Love is more than a word it's complete with action.

Love Is Art

To my loving supportive family and friends that pushed me to follow through with this. Also, to my grandmother who passed away February 8, 2018, and to anyone who has inspired me through the hurt and pain they've place upon me while they were a part of my life. There's nothing more beautiful than a broken-hearted person who mends themselves together through the art of poetry.

R.I.P. Nana.

Messiah Brown

Can an Angel Fit?

Let me inside of your mind,
How much of me can you fit inside of you?
I'll live inside of you to discover what you're looking for.
You're just like a spark but lost in the dark.
When did you get so hallow?
Tell me what you need.
All good things they say, never last.
Where did the love inside of you go?
They say love isn't love until it's past.
Tell me your secrets.
Ask me your questions.
Let me inside your mind,
How much of me can you fit inside of you?
Take me into your darkest hours.
I'll understand what hides in the shadows of your mind, I would never judge your journey.
What did you expect?
Not shy of a spark, or what hides in the dark.
I'll guide your heart,
But first, how much of me can you fit inside of you?

Blue Moon

You could be a rising sun.
A conversation under the full moon.
The pulchritudinous that leaves them in awe.
Why hide what you've been blessed with?
Why seek what you've been given at birth?
Love lives inside of you.
Exquisiteness is what you craft.
So why question what the outsiders can't understand?
When people like you only come once in a blue moon.

Love is a Meadow

Love is a meadow
That some lived to see and speak.
With care a lily will grow
With the right weather a tree will bloom vividly green.
Time takes its role encouraging everything to grow.
Water is the mirror to the universe.
Water is the purity to the earth's soul.
Sun is the beauty that illuminates upon the meadow.
Uprising from smothering clouds,
Uplifting from ignorance that ties us down.
Its warmth is the vital care that enables the bloom of the lily.
The meadow is full of life.
And what was once dull, and dank can be vibrant again.
Where there's love there's always hope.

Summer Rain

It's heavy, yet so delicate.
Lovely, yet so somber.
Oh summer rain,
I'm soaked in your tears, do angels cry to wash the lands and nurture its soil?
When lightning strikes is it you who reminds us of your might?
Oh summer rain,
the smell of you leaves a bona fide sensation; that melts into my membrane.
Touch my skin with your markings of substantial drops.
Oh how I love the smell of you.
Moist like a rainforest, the humidity arises and it feels sticky in the air;
I can almost taste you as you fill my lungs.
Oh summer rain,
you are the most sterling smell and taste in the apple city of sin;
you make my heart flutter with hope when you shine your rainbows during your showers.
I feel rejoiced with your abundance;
I'd lose myself in the clouds of heaven to dance along your sky and to see you paint it from beginning to end.
Is it a formula for hope?
Or a message for those who are lost looking for hope?
I find myself underneath your rainbow each time sighing of relief that you're up there watching over us.
That you hear my cry from inside that I hide on the outside.
Oh summer rain,
I love the beauty that you bring to wash away my pain.
Your rainbows teach me to smile again.
Oh summer rain,
you are the utopian of my summer.

Tonight

I'm like a bedroom in your eyes,
My legs tightly wrapped around you as you feel safe in a warm space inside of me.
A comfort zone you never want to leave.
The ardor we share won't leave you deceived.
Let's create something we'd both want to believe.
Friction between your pelvis and mine, thrusting in a harmonious union.
Both of us reaching a climax, to a point of no return.
You and me, face to face.
I want to be all you desire, allow me to be the match to your fire.
Passion has sparked between us,
Now here we are in this room.
Let's take advantage of the delicious secrets we have to offer.
Grab me close, kiss me hard as we fall into one another.
I'll catch you and coddle you with sensual pleasure.
Like THC is to weed.
I'll be all that you need.

Chamomile & Caffeine

The touch of your skin helps me breathe you in.
Tasting your lips give a rush I want to be in.
A moment with you is like a cup of coffee every morning, your presence is essential.
I'm at ease and on edge all at once.
When I look at you I see a story in your eyes.
Our story began with eyes locking and lips knocking.
Your hugs are like chamomile with honey soothing my anxiousness I feel when I'm in your arms.
My body shivers with fever but my soul is at ease.
You hold my hand to ensure my thoughts of what we are becoming, you leave me with no doubts that you are really here with me in this moment.
Chamomile and caffeine, you're like an excitement with a touch of peace.

September

The waxing of autumn arises as the leaves begin to dance in the wind and touch the concrete.
Leaves spread at your feet, the ground is full of vivid colors of September.
Summer leaves a bittersweet ending to a fresh start of a new beginning.
Autumns scent is in the air.
The trees are becoming bare, leaves fall one by one, twirling everywhere.
Pull out the sweaters and join the dance as the leaves fall into the autumn weather.

Heart to Heart

If there's ever an issue, I'll keep my heart open to you.
I won't forbid you nor abandon you.
I'm here for you,
If you just see instead of look you'd open yourself fully to me.
To have come this far to know, what if? Could've been true.
What if, could've became you.
What is purpose if you don't pursue?
How do confront love with covetous surrounding your liberty to feel what man is made to believe.
Desire for love isn't true love,
You can't desire what you should already feel.
You can't abuse what is of you.
Love don't love no one, so how would it know you.
It feels us,
It drugs us,
It kills us,
It heals us.
And no matter what it'll always out live us.
Time passes by, and pain becomes a memory.
Wounds become badges to life's experiences.
But love will always be a on the loose.

Checkmate

Like an open wound filled with sea salt, slowly but surely the stinging sensation will inflame into something worst.
The blood in the cut bleeds a salty red that only an angel's touch can heal.
I'll kiss you and my bruised heart will touch your tainted love.
Let's dance on the chessboard, minds going round and round until the carousel breaks down and only one of us will say checkmate.
Once you by a ticket into this temple you'll find yourself in my labyrinth.
Only one gets to walk away with their heart filled with desire setting your mind and soul on fire.
Can you find the sun in this maze?
Can you conquer love, or will this dance leave you in a lifelong daze?
I've already danced with the fool of hearts and the clowns who always asks me to stay.
The night the bloody sun rises, will you be the king of hearts?
Or just another joker lost on a carousel? Will you be the one I want to stay close to? To watch the storm rage while we take our last kiss watching the days end forever before judgment day hits us and we no longer have to live within judgment of mankind.

Cleopatra I

Shimmering lights,
Aren't you just the sweetest delight?
Whenever we're close enough we both run from one another and take flight.
Like sweet juice I just can't get enough of you.
Yeah, I know you,
Always running around sharing my gold juice.
Got me looking for you in all these hints and clues left by you.
What is it with you?
Why can't you be like the others?
Simple and easy.
But then that would make you sleazy.
I want to watch you as you get dressed before entering into the pyramids,
Jesus, how long does it take you to get ready?
What is with you, with this slow and steady?
Who is it you're trying to impress if it's not me then it must be him!
Who is he?
What's his name?
Oh, so you're just doing this to receive fame?!
So what was I?
Just another number in your love game?
Why am I not the one in your eyes?
What do you see in these other guys?
You bring out this sensual flame in me,
I'm yearning for your love!
Why?!
You play these games and have them men going crazy over some fantasy you plan to never fulfill.
Got me looking like I'm the one who sinned.
You've changed me.
I'll never forget you, or what you've done.

Cleopatra II

Would you still adore me with my hands wrapped around your neck?
The tension in this place is beyond what I'd ever expect.
They hate what I've done.
Oh well,
I'll just return them with saccharine gifts.
I told you,
I'm like the sun.
I'm warm,
I'm bright,
I'll give you a clear vision of insight.
But I burn like a mighty flame,
And sadly, I can't be tamed.
I'm wild you see,
Your lucky star.
Only I can control me.
What's done is done.
And honestly no one won.
But you can't say it wasn't fun.
I hope that when you look at the sun,
I'm the one who crosses your mind.
Don't ever look for me in the next one you meet.
Because the next one won't be able to compete.
If only you knew that every clue I gave to you, was never a lie.
It was a fantasy I made personally for amusement.
I never wanted anyone to cry.
I never expected to so many heads to pry.
I didn't promise I'd fulfill everything,
You were just too dull-witted to comprehend.
There were no sins, in this game we've played.

There were no wins.
Just a lot of clucking hens.
But hey,
I understand.
You can't always get what you want, but you'll always get what you need.
And sadly, I don't believe that'll be me.

Beast

Never let him insinuate into your comfort zone for he'll become your beast of burden.
He dazzles you with false promises and charming words to woo into opening your door.
He keeps knocking,
Why does he keep knocking?
The consistency he has, makes you question and wonder if he'll mean what he says, but he means nothing of what he says.
He doesn't even stand for himself, so why would he stand for you?
He'll just trick you into opening that door just to humiliate you, and watch you perish like you're the joke.
When you're the one who was praised.
Praised for your creativity and honest toil.
He pulls out your darkest emotions and takes away the glory you've built within you're past devastations.
Now you question your self-purpose and you doubt you're quality when you were fine before he came knocking at your door.
He's still knocking, waiting for you to open.
Don't.
All he'll do is bring forth the fury that hides within you.
God would never send something like this to you, it's a life trap.
Don't fall for anything that will never stand tall with you at you're worst.

Do You Remember?

The look in your eyes provoked an affectionate moment, which haunted my memory.
Do you still remember the first day you saw me?
Who knew love could be so poisoning. It left a feeling of nightshade.
Disparaging one another's name, we forgot our first kiss.
Do you remember the feelings that overwhelmed you when I walked towards you?
I imagined something greater than me and you.
Something heaven would smile upon and angels would cry to see it fall apart.
Don't you remember the blissful feeling between our lips?
Maybe I was a delusional believer to the whims of a LOVE without envy.
Of LOVE without the scars that comes after the big fall.
Maybe I was foolish to think that'd I'd be able to handle all the attributes that comes with being with you.
Or even understanding you.
You're a beast I can't tame.

Beauty behind the Door

There's something so beautiful about a broken heart.
The way the heart beats afterwards is like a clock ticking to be noticed from the damage.
Once the heart has been broken it adapts to understanding the lesson of what time and forgiveness should be once you listen to what that broken tick sounds like.
That's when you'll know what recovery is. And rekindle love that'll follow you like your own shadows do every day.
That's the beauty of a broken heart. Living through the pain to tell the story of what it feels like.

Broken Beat

Here I stand outside these gilded doors pondering on dreams I don't believe I'll fully receive anymore.
Your aura clashes into mine, and my heart skips to an awkward beat.
Looking down at my feet, I'm left with a disappearing bleat.
I've never felt this kind of defeat, it left me with a broken beat.
That I'm still learning to mete.
It was like rakes digging into my skin while the dead cells scattered all over the jungles concrete.
The maltreatment tasted like blood.
My blood!
I was lying in a pool made by the fool in me.
I gave Love permission to kill the angel in me, so I could see the child inside me break free from golden shackles locked away in my memories.
I stand outside these gilded doors pondering on dreams I used believe in before I reached this point.
Now I'm here making things as the hours go by waiting on them gilded doors to open.
Dreams are coming to me as, time ticks to the broken beat I keep to remind me of what I've reaped.

Seven: Thirty

Closed my eyes for a second and this wasn't what I was expecting.
His cold hands covers my mouth, and my voice is manipulated into turning off.
Chocking on words I cough up to let out falls on deaf ears.
Am I enslaved by obsession?
Is this all misled perceptions?
What I have to say sounds crazy,
How I perceive this control over me is apprehensive.
It's never ending to what exempt I'll be subjected to for this man's pleasure.
Deceived my esteem by clouded promises, which I'm supposed to believe you'll keep.
I'm crazy for having hope in who you were selling me to believe.
His cold hands compresses my tongue from speaking my truths.
I'm not eligible to be who I am because it'll only provoke him to hold me down.
My trauma strokes his ego,
If I bend backwards I'll break myself all over again.
If I speak too boldly I'll be a humiliated puppet on display.
Animosity weights on the situation, and I have nothing to show forth but agony and rage towards a man who'll never care to give me closure to pain he wanted to implant in my memory.
He keeps me reminded he's around somewhere lurking in the shadows of other people's presents.
He speaks through them,
He watches me through their eyes.
Taunted by an obsessive man who refuses to let me go.
I'm shackled to a nightmare I can't find my way out of.
Tied to a web of confusion and betrayal.
My time was raped from me.
Lost in *seven: thirty,* I've just began recovering what was stolen.

Black Beauty

I was born with a blessing and curse.
Beauty is so misunderstood, those who have it aren't usually the happiest and those who want it only seem to like to abuse it.
I developed rage as a defense method, like a beautiful rose with the sharpest thorns you'll bleed from within one touch.
Like hot ice I am tempting to touch but hard to endure.
All this rage I mask behind beauty, and all I can do is wait like an orca waits to kill its prey.
Soon they'll feel what I feel.
Soon I'll just look back at this as steroids to my strength and I'll smile as they perish in their choices they've made.
Soon I'll be his torture chamber that'll forever be implanted in his heart and trapped in his memories.

Recovering Time

Running on a treadmill towards something bigger than me.
I see what I can be,
I see what part of me is no longer.
I'll keep what's needed for this run.
Memories are like faded pictures,
You pull them out to remind yourself of times you were once a part of what no longer exists in your present moment.
Bruises become blessings,
Blessings creates new memories.
Moving mountains bigger than me,
Maybe someday I'll see myself as something greater than what I seek.
Flustered times I defeated,
Became the muse behind what I created.
Running on my own clock,
I returned all broken watches that stopped tick-toking,
And slowed my running paste and began walking.
Catching my breath,
I've finally caught myself at a right timing.
Who am I this time?
My power comes from broken beats that I said I'll defeat,
I record history from what I capture.
I create the time I exist on this earth,
And I map out the rights and wrongs along my storyline because I am one with my time.
I'll break my own heart and mend it again.
I'll fall in love and fall out of love.
Life is my time capsule that I create into fantasies that'll rip me apart as much as it fuels me with passionate flames I'll dance in till my time is left.
I live by what my heart says, and I fall in love by what my mind captures.
Time recovers by my expression of what I've captured.
Nothing's ever wasted if it was worth running on your mind at some time.
No one stays broken,
We all recover in time.

Dolls

I come from a dollhouse, where it's gorgeous to look at from the outside,
But when you look through the curtains you see imperfection and broken joints; with tainted souls.
And yet I toil through these broken emotions and drink the dirty wine of my family sins, to bleed it blue.
I tell myself not to doubt that I'll ever be like you, in order to challenge my character as the monster that was created from this tree we burn from.
I come from a selfish kind of love, filled with manipulation, deception and loneliness.
I was loved by a mother genuinely and psychologically enslaved by hers.
I was the heart of the family making it so easy to rip me apart.
Others couldn't see me for I what was but for who they wanted me to be.
I became numb to what I yearn for the most as human being, love.
I come from endless violence and emotional abuse.
I've witnessed more arguments, than I've witnessed hugs.
Hug me, and I tense up.
Love me, and I freeze.
Kiss me, and I'll be gone before your eyes open.
So I ask, what do you see when you look at me?
Am I your doll?
Am I fun for the mean time and when the next best thing comes along I'm easily disposed of?
Can you replace my grueling memories, where I shine like the sun in your hearts again?
I ask because I come from an emotional expendable family, that I chose to seek out in search of true love within the quest of recreating my own family morals and values.
So if my love comes across as plastic, or distant.
It's not.
Don't misconstrue what you shouldn't experience as a human spirit.
It'll only create the monster that'll forever remind you of the dollhouse with the family burning tree.

Mirrors

Who am I to you now?
Am I what you're used to viewing every morning, or the new you?
I ask this in honor of what you've gone through.
Has reality shown you ugly sides of me you can't bear to see?
Have you accepted those ugly truths?
I only inquire to understand you more than what I did the year before.
I stand here before you as your inner image, I give you what is of virtue.
And you still hide the greatest parts of you.
Open the door to me, and I'll set you free.
I'll bring out all the stars that you suppress inside you.
Together we'll grasp the dreams you've imagined as a child and galvanize them into your reality.
There's a verisimilitude of creativity flowing within your blood.
Whatever you think you can obtain you can receive, and if you can't get it physically, then you'll create it from nothing.
Your embodiment of me, is what makes you deadly.
It's your gift to life.
You kill, and they never forget you.
Now, who am I to you?

The Seasons of Our Heart

Dedicated to my Lord and Savior who gave me these poems to provide to you.

D.P. Parsons

SWEET MEMORIES

Sweet memories of a child still linger in my heart
Along with his smile, may they never part.
I held him in my arms, then he went away,
For the angles came for him and took him one day.
Bitter tears I cried, from the bottom of my heart,
For I sipped from the cup, though I wanted no part.
In anger I questioned, why he went away
Bringing shame to my soul, that still haunts me to this day.
For who am I to question, or ask the reason why?
For I know up in Heaven, he shall never die.
But the answer came swiftly, from my father up above
So sweet was his answer, so sweet is his love!
Lift up your heart and wipe those tears away
For he's living with me this very day.
He was never yours to give or take away
Though I let him stay awhile to brighten up your day.
Sweet memories of a child still linger in my heart
Along with his smile, may they never part.
(Dedicated to my grandson: Dylan Andrew Parsons 9/2/2002-10/18/2002)
D.P. Parsons

TOGETHER AGAIN

Upon a shelf all covered with dust,
In a cardboard box, were some pictures of us!
Memories from the past that got lost along the way,
Yet with one little glance, I'm back there today.
I can't remember how long it's been
But Lord, it felt so good, to go back home again.
Memories from the past, each one solid gold,
As I turn the pages, they go walking through my soul.
They will always be there, till my journeys end
Then up there in Heaven we'll be together again.
D.P. Parsons

CHARLIE BOY

His name is Charlie Boy, want you please take him home?
Every man needs a dog he can call his own.
Just promise me you'll love him and teach him not to bite.
He won't cost you much money, and someday I'll make it right.
I was just outside of Chicago, the rain was pouring down,
It was there in a phone booth, just outside of town.
In a cardboard box, staring up at me
Was a little sad eyed puppy, as cute as he could be.
Now he seemed so frightened, sitting there alone
But when I picked him up he knew he'd found a home.
His name is Charlie Boy, want you please take him home?
Every man needs a dog, he can call his own.
Just promise me you'll love him and teach him not to bite
He won't cost you much money and someday I'll make it right.
Now my tears fell like rain, as onward I read,
The things in this note, that my own son had said.
My momma she left us six months ago,
She went to live with Jesus and we miss her so.
Then daddy started drinking and leaving us here alone
Now, me and Charlie Boy, we don't have a happy home.
I hate to give him up, he means so much to me
But I know he deserves more, like a happy home.
His name is Charlie Boy, won't you please take him home?
Every man needs a dog he can call his own.
He won't cost you much money and someday I'll make it right.
Just promise me you'll love him and teach him not to bite.
Now it's been three long years since that stormy night,
When I threw away my bottle and tried to make things right.
My son and Charlie boy, they're as happy as they can be.

Since we moved to our new home, right here in Tennessee.
His name is Charlie Boy, won't you please take him home?
Every man needs a dog, he can call his own.
He won't cost you much money and someday I'll make it right.
Just promise me you'll love him and teach him not to bite.
(Dedicated to Blackie, Toto & Charlie Boy)
D.P. Parsons

A SOUTHERN MAN

They're saddles are all dusty, the soldiers are now gone
The cannons lie still that once rocked our homes.
In these great states of the Carolinas and Tennessee
Grand old Virginia, they're all part of history.
My forefathers fought and died for the rights to live here in this land
And I'm standing here a proud Southern man!
It's born in my blood and written in the sand
You can call me a rebel but I'm a proud Southern man.
I've lived in them all, the Carolinas and Tennessee
Grand old Virginia, they're all a part of me.
I'm just a Southern man and that's what you're gonna see
And here I stand, for this land is part of me.
D.P. Parsons

IM TOUCHED BY HIS SPIRIT

I'm touched by his spirit, so soothing to my soul
Like cool running waters over hot burning coals.
His love and his mercy shall last through the end
For I've been pardoned, he forgave all my sins
Now I know I'm not worthy of anything he's done
But God made a way when he sent me his son.
I'm touched by his spirit so soothing to my soul
Like cool running waters over hot burning coals.
His love and his mercy shall last through the end
For I've been pardoned, he forgave all my sins.
And to all I plead guilty, to everything I've done
But my God mad a way when he sent me his son.
Touched by his spirit so soothing to my soul
Like cool running waters over hot burning coals.
His love and his mercy shall last through the end
For I've been pardoned he forgave all my sins.
D.P. Parsons

MY REDEEMER

He's my redeemer, my savior and guiding light.
So pure and perfect he's everything that's right.
My bridge over troubled waters, my shelter from the storms
He holds me so close as I rest in his arms.
Thank you, Lord Jesus, for everything you've done.
Thank you, dear God, for sending your son.
He walks my path before me, as I travel on
And with each step I take, I'm a little closer home.
When my life is over all finished and done
May I walk through Heaven's gates praising God's son.
For he's my redeemer, my savior and guiding light.
So pure and perfect, he's everything that's right.
D.P. Parsons

HE ALWAYS WILL

On this road we're traveling on, we see it everyday
Troubles and trials, they keep coming our way.
Now we could turn to the left or maybe to the right
We could even try hiding in the darkness of the night.
But at the break of day, we shall find it still
It keeps hanging around and I guess it always will.
Then the sun rises up shinning once more
And there's a brand-new day like we've never seen before.
For he's our strength when we're walking in the center of his will.
And he'll be right there as we climb the next hill.
For he has always loved us, and he always will.
D.P. Parsons

GOD THE FATHER

It hurts so much, this pain inside.
The thought of you leaving, brings forth a feeling that I can't hide.
For we did so much together in what little time we had
Every memory I cherish, though some were a little sad.
We crossed many a river, and many valleys we've walked through
And the sweetest thing of all is I walked them with you.
So when I heard the news, I felt so alone
But I was so foolish, and I was so wrong.
For I knew when you left us, you took your journey home
Your rightful place in Heaven, there around God's Throne.
Where life shall never end, and no one feels alone
For God's the best father a child has ever known.
D.P. Parsons

NO PLACE TO HIDE

Now you know you can run but there's no place to hide.
And when I get a hold of you, I'm going to tan that hide.
Now living in the country, I was happy as I could be.
But many times, in my childhood, these words were spoken to me.
And as I grew older I began to understand
I was still a boy who thought he was a man.
Now you know you can run but there's no place to hide
And when I get a hold of you I'm going to tan that hide.
Now many years have passed, and both of my parents are gone
And sometimes in my heart I feel so alone.
Then my mind takes me back to another day
And I can still hear these voices as they look at me and say
Now you know you can run but there's no place to hide
And when I get a hold of you I'm going to tan your hide.
D.P. Parsons

THE KEEPER OF MY SOUL

Inside a wooden casket placed in a vault of steel
They're trying to lock me in, but they never will.
For the one who once lived there has took their journey home
Never to hurt no more or ever feel alone.
I'll pass through the darkness through the shadows of death
But only for a moment as I take my last breath.
Now there's little that I know or even understand
But I know I'll be living over in the promise land.
Over in the promise land where the milk and honey flows
Through those gates of pearl and all well with my soul.
As I go walking on those streets of gold
And there stands the master, the keeper of my soul.
D.P. Parsons

BEST FRIEND

Daddy loves the baby, momma loves it too.
We try to make it happy in everything we do.
Sometimes she gets so frightened at every little sound
And you can hear her pause a running as all four hit the ground.
Five years she's been with us and blessed us with her love.
God's beautiful creation sent down from above.
Now it feels so good to have a best friend
One who will love you, till the very end.
D.P. Parsons

CUPID

Now Cupid shot an arrow from his magic bow
Straight through my heart and it wouldn't let go.
Sending crazy thoughts straight to my head
I wish I had listened to what my daddy said.
I can remember back when I was a child
They would look at me then they would smile sending crazy thoughts straight to my head.
I wish I had listened to what my daddy said
He would look at me and say young man
Run the other way as quick as you can.
One day they'll catch you like your mother did me
And they won't let go through all an eternity.
But I never listened to what my daddy said.
I let all the young girls go straight to my head.
Now I was out with one just the other night
And when we kissed, I felt the lightning strike.
I knew it was over I was finished and done
My legs were so weak I couldn't run.
Now Cupid shot an arrow from his magic bow.
Straight through my heart and it wouldn't let go.
Sending crazy thoughts straight to my head.
I wish I had listened to what my daddy said.
D.P. Parsons

MY LAST RIDE

Let me dream of another morning when all things are set aside.
I'll have no pains no more sorrows no more fears for me to hide.
For death shall come like the darkness as I take my last ride.
But sure as day comes after the darkness
There's nothing there for me to hide.
For I know I've been forgiven and his blood has been applied
So when the dawn breaks in the morning he'll be right there by my side.
And we shall go on together as I take my last ride.
Let me dream of another morning when all things are set aside
I'll have no more pains no more sorrows no more fears for me inside.
D.P. Parsons

SERVING NINETY-NINE

Now they placed me in a prison they locked me in a cell
And there set a man who I'd get to know real well.
He said I have a number, it's stamped on my back
But in my younger days all my friends called me jack.
Now twenty years might seem like a very long time
But you could be like me serving ninety-nine.
Now I can't remember just how long it's been
Since I spoke to my wife or saw my old friends.
They used to come and visit me every weekend
Then they just stopped, and I can't remember when.
The days drag on by, as I sit here in this cell
And God only knows how many tears have fell.
But when the night time comes I'll open up this cell
And take me a trip to a time I knew so well.
I guess I was nine or I could have been ten
But I'm telling you I was back home again.
I could see my mother as she smiled at me
And papa, if I had listened, a lot better off I'd be.
But then the morning comes with the clinging of the cells
And I know I'm right back here in this living Hell.
He said I have a number, it's stamped on my back
But in my younger days all my friends called me Jack.
Now twenty years might seem like a very long time
But you could be like me serving ninety-nine.
Now I know one night when I go back home
When the morning comes they'll find that I'm gone.
But if you'll tell them for me, Jack said fair well.
And he won't be coming back to be locked in a cell.
He said I have number it's stamped on my back
But in my younger days all my friends called me Jack.
Now twenty years might seem like a very long time
But you could be like me, serving ninety-nine.
D.P. Parsons

A PART OF ME

There's a little part of me that's dying every day
A little part of me that keeps slipping away.
Now I remember my dad, and my grandfathers too.
My mother and my brother my grandmothers were so true.
Now they're all gone those little parts of me.
Though they'll live in my heart as long as I shall be.
It started at my birth and as I walked along
I was searching for a path that would guide my soul home.
The little things they taught me the words they would say
They still bring comfort to my soul as I go from day to day.
Yes, there's a little part of me that's dying every day.
A little part of me that keeps slipping away.
But at my journeys end I know I shall find those little parts of me were so divine.
Grafted by the master, to keep me in line.
And when I walk through those gates upon Heaven's shore
I won't have to worry or wonder anymore.
D.P. Parsons

REMEMBER ME

I can see that big hammer as the nails were driven in
All the pain he bore he bore for my sins.
They nailed his hands and his feet to that old dogwood tree
Then the thief he cried out Lord remember me.
And that day in paradise, together they would be
The thief who was forgiven and my Lord who died for me.
For thirty pieces of silver, Judas sold him one day.
Then the soldiers came and took my Lord away.
They scorned and mocked him in the bible I have read.
Even placing a crown of thorns on my savior's head.
By his strips we are healed in the bible I have read.
And every drop of blood for me, my savior bled.
They took him from the cross and laid him in the tomb.
And when the stone was rolled away they found an empty room.
His burial cloth was lying there folded neatly on the bed
My Lord has risen just like he said.
He was seen up a walking on that third day
He even spoke to Thomas before he went away.
Now he's coming back some great and glorious day
And just like the thief may he hear me say
Lord remember me when you pass by this way.
D.P. Parsons

THOSE LITTLE ONES

Like tear drops from Heaven, rain was falling from the sky.
As the water trickled down on my cheek, tears fell from my eyes.
God bless those little ones who seem so all alone.
Those who seem to be forgotten inside their broken homes.
Those who can't find the love that most of us have known.
They're taken from this life, long before their time
Because of their parents who seem to be so blind.
But up there in Heaven around God's throne
They won't have to worry or ever fill alone.
For there's one thing I know that keeps me marching on
The God that I serve he's still on the throne.
D.P. Parsons

THIS OLD WHITE PINE

The sap from my limbs keep dripping like tears
From all the stories I've heard through the years.
I was placed here by God's own hands, many years ago.
I was just a tiny thing till he blessed me to grow.
And all through the years I've stood straight and tall
Never once did I bend nor have a fear that I'd fall.
The squirrel ran across my limbs each day
But I don't mind they're so happy when they play.
Then the birds flew by and set for awhile
As they sing to him I know it makes him smile.
But the biggest thrill of all is when I hear someone say
It's me again God I've come out here to play.
Then they kneel down beside this old white pine
And pour out their soul, their heart and mind.
All to a God so loving and kind.
D.P. Parsons

THE SHADOWS

The shadows from the past oh they hurt me so.
Everywhere I look I now the people know.
We were always together, we were never alone
Now I'm sitting here inside this broken home.
I've tried to forget done my best to move on
But the shadows won't let me they won't leave me alone.
Now we use to go out for a night on the town
But everywhere I go you'd follow me around.
I've tried my best to forget, but can't you see?
Everywhere I go your still a part of me.
I guess when my time comes, and they lay this body down,
I'll still see you there just hanging around.
D.P. Parsons

THESE OLD EYES

Now the sky never looked grayer, nor the leaves so dry and brown
Once our life was one big circle and everyday it went round and round.
But now that circle's been broken, and all the pieces lie scattered on the ground.
And as I look through these eyes at the darkness there's no light to be found.
Lord give me the strength to walk another day and say the words you'd have me to say.
To forgive all my enemies like you'd have me to do
And honor thy father with love so true.
Then my ears shall hear the angels sing as they have before.
And the door to my heart shall swing open as the honey flows once more.
Then everything will be much brighter then these eyes have ever seen before.
D.P. Parsons

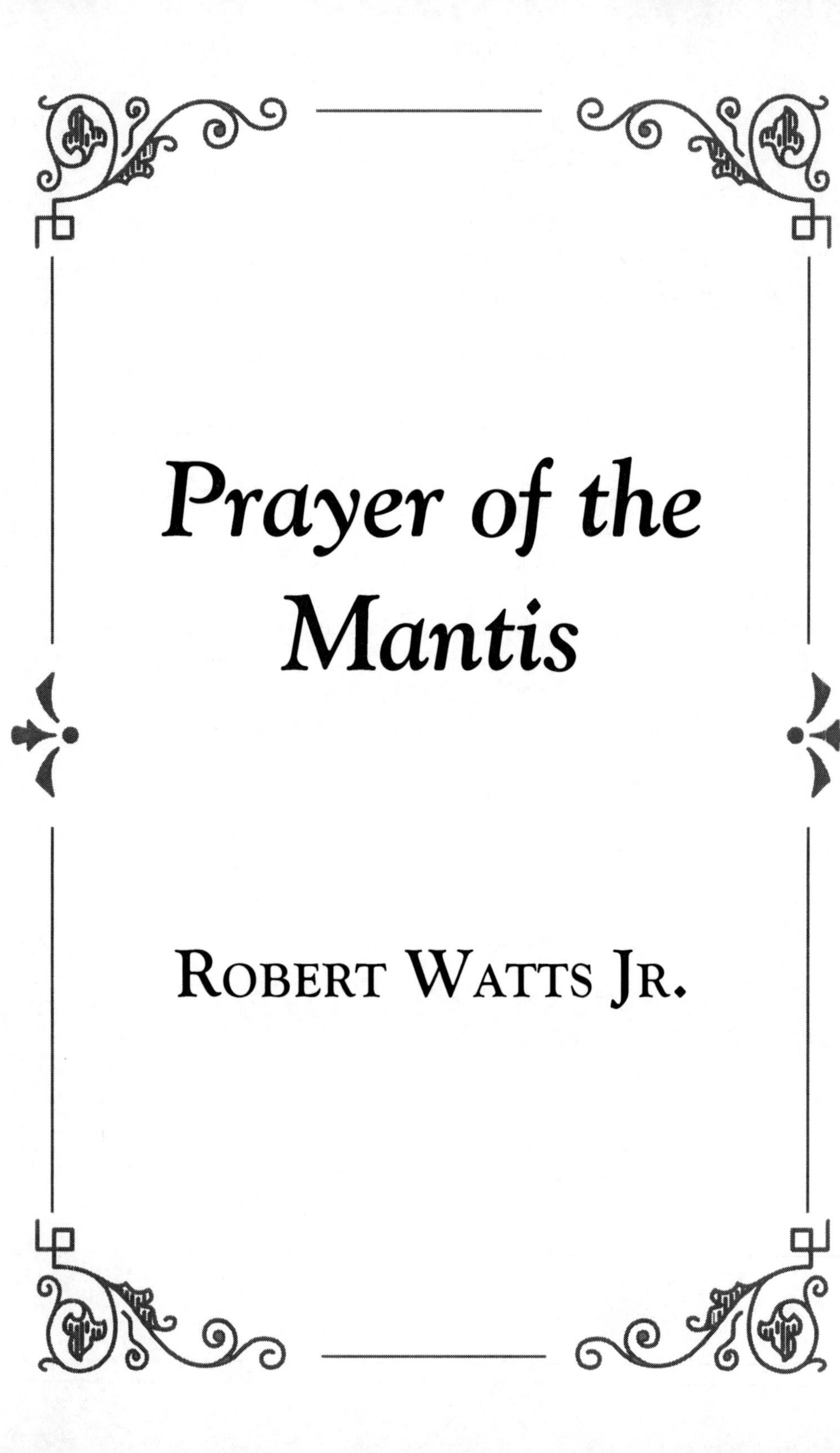

Prayer of the Mantis

ROBERT WATTS JR.

Prayer of the Mantis

(This couldn't be my partner! As scared as a kitten trapped up in a tree during a thunder storm, no this wasn't like Derrick at all. "What the fuck is going on!" I barked out at him. He attempted to paint a smile across his face hoping to camouflage his apprehensions and fear. "Big Vince thinks we're trying to play him out. Your associates on the west side are looking for us and internal affairs won't leave me alone, where the hell have you been?" "Me? What the fuck do you mean where I been?"

"Sorry man, it's just…" he began and then sat there frozen in a state of pure panic. "Sgt. Sullivan spoke to you?" The question rolled from my lips in a nice and even tone. Derrick then began to regain some composure, but I knew he was still shook. "A…yea we talked for a minute or so." "About?" He answered me with complete silence and that said it all. He cracked, and he reeked of guilt.

"Look man don't worry the money can't be traced back to the source, even if it could who're they gonna believe us or known gangsters, what'd you say to Sullivan?" Still he said nothing. "I need a drink" he muttered. "That makes two of us, man." I said freeing cigarette smoke from my tar covered lungs. Pulling my trusty flask from inside my jacket I drained it completely, and then offered it to Derrick; my partner from middle school, my best and only friend! He took it with a look of total relief blooming across his worry ridden face and as he turned up the flask and realized it was empty, I began to empty my revolver into him. The look he gave me was a look of regret and shock, of gratitude and empathy.)

That look, that whole scenario, ravages my head whenever I dare to sleep, and I blame Sullivan. Oh, he's got one coming! The racist coward! "Damn it Derrick you simple son of a bitch…"

I've killed a few people and shot even more. Killing has never bothered me that is, until Derrick. Thank God for insomnia: watching my days bleed into one another through apathetic eyes, I've realized life's irrelevance. What does it matter if one leads a good wholesome life or follows a darker path ripe with ill will and apocalyptic ambitions? "If there's truly nothing new under the sun, then what difference does making a difference really make? Life is laughable..."

As Cerise lay there perfectly still across the smoky gray satin sheets motionless like a praying mantis. I wondered if she was really asleep or just waiting for me to get up first. She's such a vision of beauty and intelligent but such a waste. She could have easily been a doctor, politician, or a model. Nations have fought wars to gain the favor of such women instead...such a waste.

Sitting up on the bed I felt the backs of her soft hands slide over my shoulders and down my chest. Gently her hands rested on my lap and slowly opened to reveal my wedding ring and badge. "Want one for the road detective Jones?"

Couldn't keep myself from grinning slightly, I nodded, and she poured. "Do I have to wait another week to see you again?" I stood up and put my pants on in response. "Here, call the shop and tell him I'm on my way." As she slides my phone open I watched in absolute stillness knowing that I'd never feel her delicate touch again. No one would.

She should have stayed in school; instead she's calling in her own hit. "There's no answer Detective," she said, handing me the phone. Sad as it may sound, in order to not fall for this one. I say as little as I can to her; she's just a little too dangerous to love. "Until next time then..." I smile and toss her a wad of cash. "Give the Mrs. my best." She hissed slithering into her dress. "Cerise honey, jealousy is just not your color." I voiced through my teeth closing the door behind me, knowing that mine was the last voice she'd ever hear. See she knew too much about me, about Derrick's disappearance, the money, everything. It's really not that hard to put together. She's a sharp one indeed. I found little solace in knowing she wouldn't suffer long, very little...but out of her or me based on what she may or may not know...well it won't be me. You do the math.

Stepping outside into the night, the lights of my neon jungle race to embrace me. I walked across the rain-soaked pavement into my personal oasis of decadent debauchery and nocturnal bliss. The city really shows her teeth at night in the rain. I love it. My fall from grace was my nefarious ticket to freedom in excess for the price of my conscious and peace of mind. In hind sight however, I'm beginning to believe that I got gypped and I seriously doubt that there's enough of me left to even care anymore.

The Source

All hail the crimson colored queen, and her ether opus
Me, I'm simply hopeless watch as she approaches
Beauty so atrocious in music so ferocious
It's impossible to cope with
This vixen's so vindictive, Pray her spells are lifted
And though I despise her absence
As much as her presence
I'm drawn to study her essence
And I value these lessons
Her dowry's quite unpleasant,
Are her melodious transgressions?
My harmonious indiscretions'
See hers' are the darkened darts that have pierced my heart
I am her mark
She's more than my match or counterpart
And that's why I'm torn apart, between the love and the art
My muse is amused by my poignant discourse
Our merciless intercourse is, my repentant source

The City

I called her Jupiter, but she was more like Bermuda

She cast shadows like smoke dancing of the cherry tips of lit incense

Amazing

I loved her because I knew she would never truly love me

She vindicated my habitually insecure inhibitions

She taught me to taste the rain and I sacrifice myself

Constantly over her satin alter where pain and pleasure

Blend like two lovers enthralled in passion's malignant cocoon

Together we composed exquisite contrast in perfect form

Pristine lines, flow, sounds, and signs

Written in the hearts most cherished chamber

She stole what was hers' to begin with as I chose to forget
To lay claim to what was rightfully mine she watched my

Soul drift off towards the beyond, then
she drew me with her chalice

Poured me into her palace then with transcendent hands she began

Caressing my face and blighting my grace

The city tastes like spit as it escapes my lips

Sick and remiss as the love I get when we kiss

My euphoric mistress, my love less goddess, the city

The Empty

I tell my streets "Sleep easy." when the morning sun kisses the skies
Day walkers stir and rise I slowly close my bloodshot eyes
To disregard what I despise, the mother of all my lies
I rambled risky in the heat of the heart of the night
Running among her young and we attack on sight
In this feverish festival of a thousand appetites
All walks of life race down these flights
Till they ascertain that act right
That they sought out round mid-night
Or get caught up in the black lights
Or the red and blue berry satellites
As pandemonium's black and whites
Snatch them down from their twisted heights
In spite of who's wrong or right?
To carry them off, and out of sight
The stunningly stoic moon simply shines and observes
As we transact and transfer like transient blurs
Misguided by expensive mixtures, toxic textures and exotic pleasures
Temptations run ramped, they run us amuck
Till we get sick, get stuck, get ghost or get plucked
As we solicit strange luck blow on the dice
That's the price we pay, the sacrifice of a new day
To sleep yesterdays levity away,
And it's resulting disarray.
The empty is the alpha and the omega.
The empty's the deity of the night children's favor
For its passionate yet fleeting feelings and immaculate lies
Opening my rapacious eyes for tonight's deceptive prize
Again my day begins with a perfect sun set and moon rise

Prayer of the Mantis

(Part II)

Walking into the corner store I see Pablo. He always has a fresh pot of extra strong coffee, gum and cigarettes waiting for me. In return I always have some of the latest narcotics raid for him. We get along fine. Once I'm completely satisfied that my breath is covered I head into the office. Turning on the lights reveals my desk covered with letters. So emptying what's left in the flask I push the letters into the trash can. One of them caught my eye.

The handwritten envelop read, "*Detective Mantis*". It was yet another letter from Derrick's widow, which will never be opened or answered. The alarm clock Derrick got it for me when I made detective went off; it felt like a bad omen. Not that I'm very superstitious, that's just how it felt. The song that the clock radio was playing has to be my all-time favorite. Reminded me of much easier time's yea, the good ole' day when waking up was all that really mattered. No time for nostalgic sentiments though I'm running late.

Hopping into the Crown Vic and hitting the lights I flew down main. Suddenly the clouds busted open and began pouring down rain fast and hard flooding the streets.

Out of nowhere an ambulance smashed into the passenger side of my car spinning me out into a nearby street light. Some might call it fate, but I believe that the bourbon in my blood stream might prove otherwise. "If it wasn't for bad luck…"

To Pale the Sunlight

I've developed deadly appetites, beneath the pale moonlight
The purpose of my plights', kept quite air tight
Not even I am aware it's buried deep in my stare, not that I care
And I doubt the devil would dare to follow me there
Through this kaleidoscope at the end of my rope
Where there's one huge knot, before a bottomless drop
I'm he born of the spirit, forged in the flesh
I bring life to this mess, that's the price of this quest
But there was no way I could have bought in for less
The stars watch me nightly through the mist and the clouds
As I finesse my way through tomorrow's yesterday
It's a hell of a game I play, one where the rules only exist
For those caught up in its twist
The metal I wrestle with has left veterans lifeless
It is nothing to trifle with, my pistol's sick so are its gifts
We accelerate apocalypse by orchestrating hollow tips
I guess it's the only way that I'll feel repaid
For all that I gave
Despite what I took, and I took in advance
Every last chance, that there was to take
Because none was ever given, so let's split these decisions
To keep on living, now we can both part ways as civilized men
Except then again, I'm not so sure I can
See! My destructive appetites got me, well, not thinking right
How's about we conclude this wasted life
With a blood-soaked fire fight, in the broadest daylight
Crushing the sun's hope for us with all our malevolent might
The same way we crush the moon's love for life at night
Thusly paling the moonlight
Oh, we'll give this world such a story
Grimacing and grinning in purely disgraceful glory
While our blood paints the lands and reddens the seas
We'll display ataxia in infinite degrees

So the light can now bear witness to what the dark was forced to be
Finally through our murderous debauchery and intimate anarchy
The sun will slowly fade into a stoic placid glow no longer bold and bright
And we will have half a breath left to spite the paling sunlight

Prayer of the Mantis

(Part III)

Perhaps it was the callous and condescending rains barreling down through the shattered windshield that forced my eyes open. Tearing myself away from the wreckage and managing to limp in the waist high murky rain waters to the up ended ambulance. I noticed that the driver was pinned into its dash board. Tried to open the door but couldn't. "Help…in the back…get them out…" his last words. Making my way to the back of the ambulance turned coffin, I saw two lifeless corpses floating in the pooling rain waters.

One was a young EMT drifting face down and perfectly still. "That could have been me…it should have been me!" I thought momentarily with a shrug, no such luck. My cell phone was soaked, the car's a memory, and I have no more time left to get to Sullivan. That bastard! I had I.A. in my pocket till he showed up. Now this accident has completely closed my only window of opportunity to frame him for Derrick's death. "Damn it! It's all going south…"

This growing despair was interrupted by a sudden assiduous and agonizing howl. It was the other floater desperately clinging to the gurney he was on. Hell, I had assumed he was dead too. A recondite tension began echoing the ever-present pain that consumed my broken body as I approached him. Standing there and looking down on this badly contorted man, soaked as much with his blood as he was the rain water. His face clinched tight by Deaths' imposing grip. "I…I…can't breath…h…help me" he began gasping.

My eyes started widening at the sound of that voice. He was my appointment! The one I was rushing to; Sgt. Sullivan of internal affairs! The one man that could single handedly end me is now inches away from his death. He's the reason Derrick died by my hand. Hatred is all there is in me for this man. "Sullivan?" escaped these lips as he lay there trembling and bleeding. The look that ran across his face when our eyes met forced me to bash him off the gurney and into the flood waters. That moment, watching him die, consumed my whole being.

As he drowned the rains subsided, leaving nothing but an uneasy silence. This deadly calm that surrounded me was soon interrupted by sirens. Looking across the street there were all these eyes on me, like they had been watching me the whole time, and they had.

Time ended with me there, standing over Sgt. Sullivan's lifeless corpse. The witnesses began rushing towards the approaching officers, screaming and pointing at me. I thought for a moment, "Shoot your way out!" I couldn't keep myself from grinning slightly. "How should I end my days? Ask to be forgiven or embrace damnation?"

Reaching down to my belt for my badge I felt the sharp and hot pain of gun shots rip through my chest. Now floating sideways with half my body submerged in the flood waters with both eyes open, I wondered which was filthier my blood or this greasy pooling murk. As they pulled me from the water I became overwhelmed with awareness feeling my spirit began to depart, and with my final breath I exhaled, "I apologize…Jesus? Father…please…forgive me…"

The DEAD ENDERS creed

Talent laid to waste leaves such a somber taste
I'd rather be erased than fail to keep the pace
Rather be misplaced than lose faith and face;

So tell my fellow Dead Enders that I fucking surrender
Forgetting to remember to pray, a prayer with specifics
And foolishly expecting to get lifted, off thinking so simplistic?

I feel so overwhelmed and helpless too much time has gotten away
Has our dedication to decay made us the perfect prey?
As decades of yesterday's parlay regrets to yet display;

Perpetual checkmate's a wanton fate, when forced to partake
In a game ripe with sin that one can never win,
With no hope to compete or walk away
complete we're slaves to defeat
So I live in my sleep;

What I've been and what I've seen has awarded me antipathy
In experiences beyond these four walls this geography
Beyond gravity, anatomy and astronomy beyond theology
I've lived without apology in my otherworldly odysseys
And the resulting guilt has hardened me;

Look behind my mask of incredulousness
With the enlightened eyes of dense prejudices,
I'm a null void of churning emptiness
Please avoid from turning into this;

See what was bestowed unto our nature
We owe to the creator and not to his hater;

With victory being our birthright and 20/20 hind sight
The fact we enjoy life is our commitment to fight
Whatever would snuff or light, right?

So then why is it so hard for us to go with God?
Is freewill such a hazardous gift to possess?
Is existence a test of spirit and flesh or faith and stress?
And do we stay safe or do we stay blessed?
Frankly I could care less, so yes give me death...